Children's Planning Strategies

David L. Forbes, Mark T. Greenberg, *Editors*

NEW DIRECTIONS FOR CHILD DEVELOPMENT
WILLIAM DAMON, *Editor-in-Chief*

Number 18, December 1982

Paperback sourcebooks in
The Jossey-Bass Social and Behavioral Sciences Series

Jossey-Bass Inc., Publishers
San Francisco • Washington • London

Children's Planning Strategies
Number 18, December 1982
    David L. Forbes, Mark T. Greenberg, *Editor*

New Directions for Child Development Series
William Damon, *Editor-in-Chief*

Copyright © 1982 by Jossey-Bass Inc., Publishers
                and
                Jossey-Bass Limited

Copyright under International, Pan American, and Universal Copyright Conventions. All rights reserved. No part of this issue may be reproduced in any form — except for brief quotation (not to exceed 500 words) in a review or professional work — without permission in writing from the publishers.

New Directions for Child Development (publication number USPS 494-090) is published quarterly by Jossey-Bass Inc., Publishers. Second-class postage rates are paid at San Francisco, California, and at additional mailing offices.

Correspondence:
Subscriptions, single-issue orders, change of address notices, undelivered copies, and other correspondence should be sent to *New Directions* Subscriptions, Jossey-Bass Inc., Publishers, 433 California Street, San Francisco, California 94104.

Editorial correspondence should be sent to the Editor-in-Chief, William Damon, Department of Psychology, Clark University, Worcester, Massachusetts 01610.

Library of Congress Catalogue Card Number LC 82-82179
International Standard Serial Number ISSN 0195-2269
International Standard Book Number ISBN 87589-878-5

Cover art by Willi Baum
Manufactured in the United States of America

Ordering Information

The paperback sourcebooks listed below are published quarterly and can be ordered either by subscription or single-copy.

Subscriptions cost $35.00 per year for institutions, agencies, and libraries. Individuals can subscribe at the special rate of $21.00 per year *if payment is by personal check*. (Note that the full rate of $35.00 applies if payment is by institutional check, even if the subscription is designated for an individual.) Standing orders are accepted.

Single copies are available at $7.95 when payment accompanies order, and *all single-copy orders under $25.00 must include payment*. (California, Washington, D.C., New Jersey, and New York residents please include appropriate sales tax.) For billed orders, cost per copy is $7.95 plus postage and handling. (Prices subject to change without notice.)

To ensure correct and prompt delivery, all orders must give either the *name of an individual* or an *official purchase order number*. Please submit your order as follows:

>   *Subscriptions:* specify series and subscription year.
>   *Single Copies:* specify sourcebook code and issue number (such as, CD8).

Mail orders for United States and Possessions, Latin America, Canada, Japan, Australia, and New Zealand to:
>   Jossey-Bass Inc., Publishers
>   433 California Street
>   San Francisco, California 94104

Mail orders for all other parts of the world to:
>   Jossey-Bass Limited
>   28 Banner Street
>   London EC1Y 8QE

New Directions for Child Development Series
William Damon, *Editor-in-Chief*

CD1 *Social Cognition,* William Damon
CD2 *Moral Development,* William Damon
CD3 *Early Symbolization,* Howard Gardner, Dennie Wolf
CD4 *Social Interaction and Communication During Infancy,* Ina C. Uzgiris
CD5 *Intellectual Development Beyond Childhood,* Deanna Kuhn
CD6 *Fact, Fiction, and Fantasy in Childhood,* Ellen Winner, Howard Gardner
CD7 *Clinical-Developmental Psychology,* Robert L. Selman, Regina Yando
CD8 *Anthropological Perspectives on Child Development,* Charles M. Super, Sara Harkness
CD9 *Children's Play,* Kenneth H. Rubin
CD10 *Children's Memory,* Marion Perlmutter
CD11 *Developmental Perspectives on Child Maltreatment,* Ross Rizley, Dante Cicchetti
CD12 *Cognitive Development,* Kurt W. Fisher

CD13 *Viewing Children Through Television,* Hope Kelly, Howard Gardner
CD14 *Childrens' Conceptions of Health, Illness, and Bodily Functions,*
     Roger Bibace, Mary E. Walsh
CD15 *Children's Conceptions of Spatial Relationships,* Robert Cohen
CD16 *Emotional Development,* Dante Cicchetti, Petra Hesse
CD17 *Developmental Approaches to Giftedness and Creativity,*
     David Henry Feldman

Contents

Editors' Notes   1
David L. Forbes, Mark T. Greenberg

Chapter 1. What Is Planning Development the Development of?   5
Roy D. Pea
Making a developmental perspective on planning activities explicit may be necessary not only for the formulation of a developmental psychology of planning but also for the development of planning by individuals.

Chapter 2. Planning and the Development of Communication Skills   29
Charlotte J. Patterson, Ralph J. Roberts, Jr.
A review of the literature on children's referential communication ability suggests how these studies help us understand children's planning in their social interactions with others.

Chapter 3. Preschoolers' Changing Conceptions of Their Mothers: 47
A Social-Cognitive Study of Mother–Child Attachment
Robert S. Marvin, Mark T. Greenberg
The development in patterns of separation behavior is interpreted in terms of symbolic-thought development and the increased importance of abstract plans for behavior.

Chapter 4. Children's Plans for Joining Play: 61
An Analysis of Structure and Function
David L. Forbes, Mary Maxwell Katz, Barry Paul, David Lubin
An analysis of children's strategies for joining playmates' activities reveals age- and sex-linked differences in affiliative planning.

Chapter 5. Communication and the Development of Social Role Play   81
Catherine Garvey
Communication with both caregivers and peers about pretend role enactments precedes the appearance of social role play in the third year of life.

Index   103

Editors' Notes

Making and following plans is an activity familiar to everyone; if asked, almost anyone could provide examples of how planning plays a role in day-to-day activities. Examples emerging from such inquiry would doubtless indicate the many types of planning, from planning what to eat for lunch to planning renovations on a summer house to planning career goals. In the broadest view, planning is an activity that goes on whenever an individual formulates a goal in advance of acting and then directs action in systematic pursuit of this goal. What unites all the diverse forms of planning are three central characteristics: the formulation of some goal or intention in advance; the formulation of strategies designed to bring about the goal; and the continuous evaluation of how well the strategies are working, with alterations in the plan as required.

Planning's relevance to almost every sphere of human activity has always interested developmental psychologists. Baldwin (1903) studied the development of very rudimentary plans as he observed interactions between infants and objects in the environment. His account of "circular reactions" in infant behavior described the gradual emergence of planning in the child's attempts to "make things happen" through his/her own motor behaviors. Piaget (1952) viewed the capacities to anticipate the outcomes of action and to reflect on and understand its impact as central foci of intellectual development. His accounts of emerging childhood intelligence relied on the concept of these two capacities to describe growing sophistication and purposefulness in childrens' abilities to solve problems. Bruner (1970), in his account of the acquisition of skilled action, explicitly treats the notion of planning as a central feature of development, again emphasizing the importance of the two capacities Piaget viewed as crucial to intellectual growth. Miller, Gallanter, and Pribram (1960) have developed a model that describes the basis in planning of a wide array of human activity, and they suggest that this basic planning behavior is what principally helps psychologists understand the organization of human action.

The chapters in this volume carry developmental psychologists' historical interest in planning into the more recently evolved field of children's social development. Past students of social reasoning (or "social intelligence") focused on elucidating how information about the social world was organized in the mind of the developing child and strived to describe changes in the structure of children's social knowledge over the course of development. This volume seeks to show how knowledge is applied in social situations by the deliberate orchestration of social actions aimed at particular goals. In Chapter One, Roy D. Pea reviews work by researchers who have attempted to delineate the cognitive components of the planning process, and he summarizes the available information about development of different cognitive abilities relevant to planning. Pea also presents some of his own recent data on children's understanding of planning behavior, including their thoughts about when one should plan, why planning is important, and what planning involves.

In Chapter Two, Charlotte J. Patterson and Ralph J. Roberts, Jr., examine planning as it pertains to referential communication. They also review past studies of referential communication and their impact on our understanding of how children plan communicative interactions. This review suggests that young children have the most difficulty with orchestrating component skills to meet the demands of referential communication tasks (an ability that Pea would term "metaplanning").

In Chapter Three, Robert S. Marvin and Mark T. Greenberg examine mother–child planning of separations and reunions. They provide evidence to suggest that attachment and separation issues involving concrete comings and goings in infancy and early childhood are transformed into issues of symbolic togetherness in the later preschool years, when separations are tolerable if a plan for reunion is made in advance.

In Chapter Four, David L. Forbes, Mary Maxwell Katz, Barry Paul, and David Lubin present an analysis of children's social interactions during episodes of joining in with others. They examine the development of intentional social interaction by analyzing the sequential organization of joining behavior, and they suggest how structural and functional considerations can be integrated into a developmental account of social planfulness.

In Chapter Five, Catherine Garvey explores the structure of children's social-role play and examines how the creation of joint plans for play requires a complex variety of interactive techniques, which emerge and develop during the early childhood years.

Each of these chapters has a distinct way of increasing our knowledge about the roles that planning plays in children's social lives. Chapter One provides a valuable introduction to the literature on plans and planning, which may be unfamiliar to many students of social development. The categories of the planning process that emerge from Pea's review of this literature will prove indispensable to those who wish to combine the study of planning with the study of social development. Pea's interview data on children's understanding of planning provide landmarks for much-needed investigation into how children themselves view both planning and its relationship to everyday activity. Chapter Two's review of the literature on referential communication helps integrate an extensive body of past research in social development into a perspective that highlights planning behavior. Marvin and Greenberg, in Chapter Three, provide a provocative vision of just how important planning becomes as the child develops a capacity for abstract thinking. The authors of Chapter Four demonstrate the value of a planfulness perspective for relating structure to function with regard to children's peer interactions. Finally, in Chapter Five, Garvey's study of planning in children's fantasy play helps the reader see how the world of play is an important context for learning social skills.

Despite the diverse perspectives in this volume, there emerges a core of issues that all our contributors address, and the reader should keep these issues in mind. First, the authors emphasize that skills acquisition per se is not the stuff of which all developmental accomplishment is composed; each chapter, in its own way, emphasizes the importance of synthetic, integrative functions that combine discrete abilities to meet the demands of a particular task. Second, all five chapters point to the importance of understanding how children define tasks *for themselves* in their day-to-day activities. Developing and refining goals for action emerges as an important topic for study in its own right, since these capacities are crucial to planning behavior. Understanding the relationship between children's goals and behavior patterns also emerges as a central topic for study, since identical behaviors may take on very different meanings, depending on variations in the child's goals.

For those of a positivistic philosophical bent, it can be said, at minimum, that a major function of a scientific psychological language is that it provides a means by which we can talk sensibly about behaviors as connected phenomena, by reference to some underlying construct that forges the linkage, from action to action. If human behavior did not display a certain regularity to the onlooker, if the totality of individual movements could never be synthesized into something that has meaning beyond the sum of its parts, then the entire scientific enterprise of psychology would most likely falter, if not cease altogether. The concept of planning is not new to psychology; indeed, it has performed this crucial synthetic function in numerous theoretical analyses of human action. The chapters in this sourcebook represent some beginning attempts at bringing planning out of the realm of theory and into the field of empirical study. It is our hope that this volume will both inform and provoke readers, so that we can gain some perspective on the task of creating developmental research that has understanding children's planning behavior as a central focus.

David L. Forbes
Mark T. Greenberg
Editors

References

Baldwin, J. *Mental Development in the Child and the Race, Methods and Processes.* New York: Macmillan, 1903.

Bruner, J. S. "The Growth and Structure of Skill." In K. Connolly (Ed.), *Mechanisms of Motor Skill Development.* New York: Academic Press, 1970.

Miller, G. A., Galanter, E., and Pribram, K. H. *Plans and the Structure of Behavior.* New York: Holt, Rinehart and Winston, 1960.

Piaget, J. *The Origins of Intelligence in Children.* New York: International Universities Press, 1952.

David L. Forbes is research associate at the Laboratory of Human Development, and director of the Peer Interaction Project at the Harvard Graduate School of Education.

Mark T. Greenberg is an assistant professor of psychology at the University of Washington.

Making a developmental perspective on planning activities explicit may be necessary not only for the formulation of a developmental psychology of planning but also for the development of planning by individuals. School-aged children have some knowledge about planning, but they focus very little on the central revisionary quality of plan construction and plan execution.

What Is Planning Development the Development of?

Roy D. Pea

We know very little about the development of planning, yet planning is so fundamental to the fabric of everyday experience that understanding its origins, components, and ways of developing is essential. Kaplan (1967, 1982) has emphasized how development is a concept distinct from ontogenesis. Persons not only progress but also regress, even during a single day. Different persona, stresses, anxieties, time demands, drugs, and brain injuries may all affect the developmental level of a person's planning. Since ontogenesis can be recognized as either regressive or progressive, "more developed" is a concept distinct from "occurring later in time." Development is a concept we apply to, rather than find in, persons or performances across time. Thus, we need to elucidate the criteria intrinsic to our grading of planning activities as more or less highly developed.

This chapter presents research conducted at the Bank Street College of Education and directed toward addressing these problems. Our general endeavor is to construct a practical theoretical perspective on planning devel-

The research and preparation of this chapter were supported by the Spencer Foundation. I would like to thank Leonard Cirillo, David Forbes, Jan Jewson, Bernard Kaplan, Denis Newman, Karen Sheingold, Seymour Wapner, and Sheldon White for their incisive comments and discussions concerning the material presented here.

opment, specifying what develops and how it develops, as well as indicating methods for its advancement. The focus of our empirical work is microcomputer programming in elementary school classrooms, which constitute a rich and explicit context for examining dynamic planning processes. A key goal is to provide a foundation for research by investigating the role explicit planning plays in children's lives, and one project of our planning-development enterprise is to interview children on the criteria they use to distinguish better from worse plans and planners. Analogous studies of children's awareness of their own learning processes have yielded new understandings of how metacognition influences learning (Baker and Brown, 1980). Since many children see no need for planning to solve school-subject problems, but do plan in other areas of their lives, these results may indicate pathways for generalizing everyday planning skills.

This chapter has three parts. The first part is a reflective analysis of what makes up the planning process. In talking about how planning works, we shall assume the achievement of some crucial developments, such as the ability to distinguish between constructing plans prior to action and carrying out the plans. These are central genetic themes, but our focus will be on the development of the organizational components of planning processes, and our empirical studies of planning are presented in these terms. This discussion will owe much to Wapner and Cirillo (1974), whose work has inspired these reflections on the organizational aspects of planning. The second part of this chapter summarizes our interview protocols of children's perspectives on planning. The third part describes new research directions (including our current planning-developmental studies) prompted by this analytical work.

The Concept of Planning

Planning is a complex form of symbolic action that consists of consciously preconceiving a sequence of actions that will be sufficient for achieving a goal. It is set apart from undeliberated action, which is not preconceived. "Plan construction" refers to the process by which plans are formulated and "plan execution" to the process by which plans are carried out.

Theorists of planning distinguish four general steps in the planning process:
1. Representing the planning problem situation, a task that requires the planner to
   (a) define the goal state,
   (b) define the problem state,
   (c) note the differences between the problem and goal states, and
   (d) determine the constraints on planning (space, time, and causation) that for example, redefine the goal.
2. Plan construction, requiring formulation of a plan to eliminate the differences between the problem and the goal state.

3. Plan execution.
4. Planning-process remembering.

These steps are not independent; otherwise, they could never be integrated into a functional planning process (Stefik, 1981a, 1981b).

Representing the Planning Problem

1. *Defining the Goal State.* While goal definition in lab tasks, where goals are defined by instructions, is relatively trivial (see, for example, Anzai and Simon, 1979), goal setting for most everyday planning is a major problem. Dewey (1922), Bruce and Newman (1978), and Wilensky (1981) have urged that goal definition be considered as problematic and as requiring the integration of multiple goals. The concept of goal was decisively elucidated by the seminal work of Miller, Galanter, and Pribram (1960). In their view, planning consists of configuring a series of tests and operations that will be performed sequentially to achieve the goal and then "exit" (stop) when the plan is executed (test, operate, test, exit). Goals are defined and redefined throughout the planning process (as the consequences of carrying out plans reveal emergent goal conflicts, for example).

The need for goal resolution in the planning process makes apparent the central role of principles of metaplanning. Wilensky (1981) has expressed these principles as metagoals that plans should attain, and Kotarbinski (1965) has informally set out comparable principles. Schutz (1973) has raised similar points. We have taken key aspects of these approaches to planning and derived four primary principles, or metagoals, of planning. The highly developed planner is guided by metagoals to check whether the plan is feasible, flexible, economizes action, and maximizes goal value.

Principle of feasibility. Impossible goals should be avoided, so that plans to achieve goals are feasible, but avoiding impossible goals is more difficult than it may appear. Subgoals must be consistent—so that, for example, acts necessary to achieve one subgoal do not block achievement of others; but goal possibility is often indeterminate, particularly for unfamiliar territories. The developing planner must first recognize that plans have to be feasible, regardless of the domain they concern. How feasibiity is determined is subject to great developmental variation. Four dimensions of plan feasibility, which should reveal developmental change, can be distinguished.

First, there is a need for well-defined goals. Second, there must be strategies for determining a plan's feasibility. Knowledge of the prior success of a plan or of one similar to it is the default strategy for determining plan feasibility. Classifying the planning situation as comparable or designating a previously successful plan as similar to the one being considered calls for a generative taxonomy of situations and plans that are capable of incorporating new cases. Third, when no comparable plan can be used for goal achievement, a feasible plan must be constructed, and knowledge of the world context (physical laws, social mores, and so on) plays a seminal role here. This third dimension—knowledge of the world context for the plan—provides the data for projecting the consequences of particular planning decisions. The development of techniques for plan projection constitutes the fourth major dimension of determining plan feasibility. A planner may have a richly structured knowledge base for the planning domain, but may not know or be able to use techniques for applying that knowledge to the plan-projection dimension.

It is clear, then, that mastery of the principle of feasibility involves knowing everything that will be relevant to the feasibility of the plan once it is in action. Projecting the consequences of plan execution tests the boundaries of human knowledge; even failed plans, if the planner is fully mindful of what went wrong, tell the planner something new about the world.

Principle of economy of actions. Processing resources such as attention, energy, and time should be conserved, from three perspectives on economy. Plan construction may be more or less economical, the effort to 'read' the plan during its execution may be more or less substantial, and the arrangement of plan component acts may require more or fewer resources to execute. Optimal planning activity minimizes processing resource expenditures from all three perspectives (Kotarbinski, 1965).

The development of this metaplanning principle requires cost-benefit analyses and has been a major goal of the high-risk activities of business, government, industry, and the military. Tradeoffs of resource economy from the three perspectives are difficult to conceptualize, but, unless the planner believes that the benefits derivable from planning efforts are greater than their costs, the generative planning that is a prerequisite of any comparative evaluation of plans is unlikely. One basic aspect of this principle of economy is realizing that planning resources are limited and need to be conserved. (Let us note here that an emphasis on the importance of cost-benefit analysis does not assign the values for such calculation. A value theory is also required. The abhorrent and antihumanistic consequences of some cost-benefit analyses proceed from misguided systems of values and should not be taken to indicate the inadequacy of cost-benefit analysis for decision making in general. A perfected conception of planning would integrate highly developed techniques into the promotion of highly "good" values as ends.)

Minimizing plan-construction efforts is an important facet of planning development. It is easier to apply a ready-made plan than to construct a new one, even if ready-made plans sometimes take longer to execute.

Concerning plan reading efforts, Meacham and Kushner (1980) have focused on "prospective memory" of a planned action, such as locking a door. Because of forgetting, "reading" a plan at its time of execution is problematic. Minimizing resource expenditures consists of developing such means for aiding plan "readability" as lists, diaries and help from other people. The collaborative aspects of prospective memory are known by school-aged children (Kreutzer, Leonard, and Flavell, 1975). Also, if the plan is to be "read" by others (as a blueprint or a story), it must be in a code that can be deciphered by its audience and may be more or less economical in plan "readability" (Burke, 1945).

For economy of plan execution, methods have only recently been developed to calculate optimal paths for sequencing component acts of a complex plan (for example, the PERT technique used in Polaris missile development or the "critical path" methods described by Levy, Thompson, and Wiest, 1963). With respect to everyday or school activities of children and adults, little is known about when or why resources for plan execution are minimized.

Principle of goal-value maximization. In situations where goals are in conflict, a higher-order set of compatible goals must be chosen. A goal definition should be selected to maximize the value of the goals to be achieved. This principle takes as objects the planner's defined goals and the metagoals expressed in the metaplanning principles. The planner tacitly or explicitly assigns weights to different plan outcomes and chooses a plan accordingly; setting goal values is thus a basic developmental achievement. More highly developed planning and planners would employ this principle, but many persons opt for any plan that works, not comparing alternatives for relative goal-value maximization.

Principle of flexibility. Planners should be sensitive to newly arising circumstances, and plan precision should not exceed limits of possible adaptation. To increase flexibility, planners should avoid early commitment. One should not decide on a plan feature that unnecessarily narrows the range of possibilities for plan development (Kotarbinski, 1965; Stefik, 1981a, 1981b). One also avoids rigidity by not deciding on a definite action if it depends on unknown or indeterminable circumstances, because if circumstances block the action, the plan must be abandoned.

2. ***Defining the Problem State and Noting Differences Between the Problem and Goal States.*** Understanding the problem requires the planner to determine which aspects of the current situation distinguish the problem state from the goal state. The less-developed planner may have difficulty encoding the problem situation. For example, age changes with respect to encoding and attentional processes may be partly responsible for the generally "novice like" performances of children on problem-solving tasks (Case, 1978; Siegler, 1981): Problem-encoding deficits may characterize performances in new planning domains; and situational features relevant to plan design may not be attended to for problem representation (Newell and Simon, 1972). Encoding deficiencies hamper the developmental sophistication of any planning, not only children's.

3. ***Determining the Constraints on Planning.*** A crucial aspect of representing the problem is elaborating the constraints imposed on planning. These include the time available to construct or execute the plan, the characteristics of the physical spaces where the plan will be executed, consequences

of executing parts of the plan, and availability of resources (for example, attention, working memory, processing energies, the possibility of help from other persons, mnemonic aids, and so on). Constraints frequently pose as instructions: "Classify the objects in a new way." Some constraints remain tacit until violated, but all constraints restrict the range of feasible plan designs. The goal definition is thus qualified in terms of its constraints.

Plan Construction

Potential methods for eliminating differences between the goal and problem states must be proposed and evaluated. As Polya (1945) observed, the planner first asks whether a method for solving the problem is known. This move economizes plan construction. The "script" concept of Schank and Abelson (1977) describes such rote procedures. A ritual plan can be used, failing which a modification or an entirely new plan may work.

Many alternative models of plan-construction processes have been proposed in cognitive science. Recent models of planning reject earlier assumptions that planning consists exclusively of a hierarchical, top-down process of refinement (Ernst and Newell, 1969; Fikes and Nilsson, 1971; Sacerdoti, 1977). Six fundamental points of agreement emerge from this literature.

Point 1. Formulating an effective plan requires plan simulation, the hypothetical execution of alternative plans proposed by the planner. The development of this aspect of planning may be assessed from three perspectives. The first is whether and to what extent the planner considers possible alternatives. Goldin and Hayes-Roth (1980) found that less effective planners considered a wide range of plan alternatives, whereas more effective planners, mindful of plan constraints, restricted attention to a smaller and more promising set. From our developmental perspective, the optimal range of plan formulations will depend on the values intrinsic to the planner's metaplanning principles. Quickly constructing a plan that works (and which may not be the shortest path to the goal) may be more highly valued than a shorter path achieved with greater effort and over a longer time. Second, alternative plans may be formulated, but not (or only partially) simulated in thought, so that consequences of plan execution are not well specified. The less developed planner may not simulate plans, either because of inability or because of not recognizing the need to do so. And third, the planner may perform a faulty simulation of plans, because of the operation of a different system of causal reasoning (see Bullock, Gelman, and Baillargeon, in press).

Point 2. Plan simulation is very complex, requiring knowledge of what would happen if the simulated plan were executed. Planning skills interact with the specific-content domain for planning. The principle of feasibility requires extensive world knowledge for realistic plan evaluation. This is true both during plan construction and plan execution, and so the extent and organization of the planner's knowledge will be critical factors.

The development of time-estimation abilities for component acts of the plan relates to the principle of economy of actions. More highly developed planners make more accurate estimates of the time required for planning.

In fact, Hayes-Roth (1980) found that adult planners generally underestimated time for executing plans, and that time stress makes underestimation of such time requirements more pronounced. Furthermore, lacking experience or knowledge of plan component acts for new domains, more highly developed planners would seek out the advice of knowledgable others. More highly developed planners know how to promote their own planning development; they initiate progress through their "zone of proximal development" (Vygotsky, 1978).

Point 3. Planners may become aware of new goals during plan simulations or attempts at plan execution and may redefine the goal state accordingly. Fully effective planning would not require goal redefinition, since all outcomes resulting from plan execution would be anticipated, but the complexities of monitoring consequences, as well as potential world-event contingencies that could block the success of component actions, make goals redefinition a common feature of planning. Nevertheless, the more highly developed planner needs to engage in relatively less goal redefinition. "Goal," as used here, is qualified in terms of the metagoals specified earlier. For example, planners may give up details to save time, realizing that goal redefinition may be required later; therefore, a plan only partially specifying its consequences would suffice for their purposes.

Point 4. The plan-construction process consists of cycles of proposal, simulation, evaluation, and revision, until a plan is formulated that will achieve the goal state. Plan construction and execution are each subject to continual control and revision. As plans are constructed, planners are guided by knowledge, which imposes constraints and gives direction to the evolving plan design. Similarly, as plans are executed, contingencies may arise that require revision of the constructed plan so as to ensure goal achievement. Goldin and Hayes-Roth (1980) found that greater planning effectiveness was characteristic of those planners who frequently evaluated and revised their proposals in terms of their goals and their metagoals. This finding may provide a useful developmental criterion for planning, since the cost of frequent revision, in terms of the planner's values (for example, economy) would usually be lower than the benefits arising from the better plan that would result from such revisions.

More effective planning has also been shown to be associated with a least-commitment strategy (Goldin and Hayes-Roth, 1980; Stefik, 1981a, 1981b), in which the planner avoids becoming committed to a planning decision until commitment consequences are evaluated with respect to goals. Keeping options open is the point, but it is easier said than done. The complex trade-offs between resources used to compute the consequences of early planning decisions and the value of avoiding subsequent reformulation are still to be studied. We suppose that, on many occasions, a least-commitment strategy would be more likely to ensure plan feasibility, but only with much time and energy required to project the consequences of early planning decisions.

It is clear, too, that these trade-offs depend on familiarity with the planning domain, because consequences of component acts are more easily projected for familiar domains and are therefore worth the minimal efforts of the least-commitment strategy; less familiar domains will have the high costs associated with such a strategy.

Point 5. Plan construction involves many kinds of decision making, on more or less concrete levels, that guide the flow of the planning process and select features of proposed methods. Besides the need to decide on action at the most concrete level of plan determination, four other types of planning decisions have been identified in adult planning protocols (Hayes-Roth and Hayes-Roth, 1979): "The subject makes decisions about data—how long errands should take, how important individual errands are, what the consequences of a particular action might be, and so forth. He makes decisions about abstract features of plans—what kinds of plan decisions might be useful. He makes metaplanning decisions—how to approach the problem and how to constrain and evaluate the plan. Finally, the subject makes executive decisions about how to allocate his cognitive resources during planning" (p. 305).

In one study, ineffective adult planners focused on low-level planning decisions, rarely assessing data relevant to plan construction or making executive or metaplanning decisions about plan-construction processes (Goldin and Hayes-Roth, 1980). Furthermore, within each type of decision making, the construction of a repertoire of options is a major developmental achievement. Planners may recognize that decisions about abstract features of plans would be helpful in plan construction, but they may not know what kinds of plan-design options there are, in the sense that what exists is determined by what others have already invented. A great deal of learning must take place before the planner can build up an inventory of possibilities for each of the general types of decision making that planning involves.

Point 6. The process of planning flexibly and purposefully shifts among making the different types of planning decisions in an advantageous manner. Earlier models favored a hierarchical, top-down approach to planning in which plans are fully formulated at the highest level of abstraction and then successively refined to a fully specified plan of concrete actions. Data from real-world tasks such as errand planning (Hayes-Roth and Hayes-Roth, 1979), designing genetics experiments (Stefik, 1981a, 1981b), or designing software (Jeffries and others, 1981) reveal that plan construction often proceeds more advantageously. As Hayes-Roth and Hayes-Roth note, "Current decisions and observations suggest various opportunities for plan development... [and] subsequent decisions follow up on selected opportunities" (p. 276; compare Wilensky, 1981; Stefik, 1981a, 1981b). Planning, in this more comprehensive view, may proceed in some cases (for example, menu planning—see Byrne, 1977) in terms of a define-and-refine planning strategy, but a highly developed planner has the flexibility (Werner, 1957) to choose advantageous planning strategies when they are warranted by problem characteristics.

It has been suggested that a planner proceeding advantageously needs a larger working memory than a hierarchical planner, since many decisions at different levels of abstraction have to be remembered (Goldin and Hayes-Roth, 1980; Thorndyke, 1978). Nevertheless, studies that relate working memory to planning will miss a key point of planning ecology: A planner may use mnemonic aids (for example, lists or telling friends) to remember details of the plan.

More highly developed planners would thus be flexible at selecting a planning strategy optimal both for the problem (Hayes-Roth and Hayes-Roth, 1979) and for their own self-assessed skills, being capable of shifting attention to different levels of decision making during plan construction, and calling on mnemonic devices when demands for remembering the plan exceed working memory.

Plan Execution

The development of plan-execution skills has seldom been studied. Part of this neglect derives from top-heavy models of planning processes. Research is devoted to proposing, simulating, and revising tentative plans, which are executed only when perfected. Much everyday planning appears bottom-heavy by comparison. Plans are often not self-consciously differentiated from actions. People frequently spring into action, explicitly constructing plans only if their actions do not succeed or if they have failed badly in previous, comparable activities.

When people do construct plans, how is plan execution monitored and controlled? And if a plan has faults, how does the planner correct them? In other words, how do planners integrate the processes of plan construction and execution?

The control processes for plan execution are similar to those for plan construction. Plan feasibility, economy of actions, goal-value maximization, and flexibility are projected on the basis of the world-state information that the planner considers to be germane. When the plan is executed, however, new world states may arise that render the plan unworkable. Some of these happenings may be caused by the unanticipated consequences of actions based on shortsightedness, while others are beyond the planner's purview. We expect that the observance of plan-intrinsic flaws will promote greater efforts at plan construction, while plan-extrinsic problems may be written off to the vagaries of the world and to the many interactions among its component events.

Planning-Process Remembering

Remembering the plans we have constructed is a key part of planning development, whether or not we use mnemonic aids. The planner needs a storehouse of useful methods for future goal-directed activities. Failed as well as successful plans should be remembered, and so, too, should their histories. Studies that describe the genesis of planning and subsequent recall of newly learned plans have yet to be carried out. Nelson and Gruendel (1979) have shown that preschoolers have rich "script" knowledge for activities like going to restaurants, but they have not traced the genetic route that leads from plan construction to plan execution to plan use. Case studies of planning development for new planning domains would be informative.

Summary

The need for instructional programs that guide the development of planning abilities is particularly acute, not only for school contexts, but also for everyday problem-solving activities involving career, financial, educational, and family planning. Preliminary to designing such programs is the identification of fronts on which developments may occur in component aspects of planning processes. Many of these fronts involve general metaplanning principles that are relevant to any planning domain, whereas other principles involved are quite specific, such as the extent and organization of plan-relevant knowledge. We need studies that chart how advances along the various fronts of planning-ability development are interrelated.

We suggest that metacognition drives cognition in significant ways. More highly developed planning may be facilitated when planners themselves have a developmental perspective on planning. Understanding the development of planning abilities will thus depend in part on articulating planners' own developmental perspectives on planning, as well as on probing the relationships between reflective activity and actual planning performances. As part of such an inquiry, we present here the results of a structured-interview study of school-aged children's talk about planning, and we make connections to the developmental framework we have outlined above.

Children's Perspectives on Planning

To get a first charting of conditions that may prompt planning in children, we used the clinical-interview method in our exploration of planning conceptions. We wanted to know how children define planning; what they see as occasions for planning or not planning, both for themselves and for others; how they assess the quality of plans and planners; and how they plan. We recognize the limitations of verbal reports in research on basic cognitive processes (Ericcson and Simon, 1980). Nevertheless, children's talk about planning is likely to advance our understanding of their reflective awareness of planning, its occurrences, its workings, and its functions. Our interview data therefore concern reflective rather than strategic metacognition (Brown and DeLoache, 1978); the latter is revealed in planning-task performances. In another study (Pea, Jewson, and Sheingold, forthcoming), we shall compare the interview results with planning-task performances.

In this part of the chapter, we briefly review findings from in-depth, structured interviews with thirteen eight- and nine-year-olds (younger group) and thirteen eleven- and twelve-year-olds (older group) at the Bank Street School. For each age, half the children were boys and half were girls. Children were principally middle-class, of diverse racial and cultural backgrounds, and spoke English. Almost all the children defined planning solely as thinking ahead about what to do in the future. A few children also noted that plans "can be changed" before they are done.

Prototypic Cases of Planning in Everyday and School Actitivies

If an activity is one a child believes other people plan for or have planned for in the past, the child will probably be more likely to access and use their own planning skills. When children were asked about when they and others plan, three types of responses occurred: planning to do something, planning how to do something, and planning the specific conditions of doing something.

Planning to Do Something. Planning to do something in particular can be described as goal setting. The planning occasions of this type that children reported are listed in descending order of how frequently these occasions were mentioned. (See Table 1.)

Thirty-one other activities were mentioned once. Those mentioned by younger children included going to a movie, camp, choir, a relative's house, or a summerhouse; dedicating a book to someone; lighting a firecracker; having a dance for someone; having a secret; inviting people to a wedding; and making a nuclear bomb. Older children noted plans to attach a model-airplane wing; blow up a general's car; carry in subtraction; catch robbers; do a research project; perform gymnastics; balance a bank account; escape from jail; get married; go to a baseball game, bed, dinner, swimming, swimming practice, or on a day hike; have a slumber party; have lunch; interview someone; ride a bike; and take a bath. The principal age difference was reflected not in the absolute number of activities cited (younger, thirty-seven; older, forty), but, rather, in the number of different activities (younger, twenty-one; older, twenty-nine). There was greater commonality among the younger group of those activities felt to be appropriate for planning.

Planning How to Do Something. Children recognized that one can plan not only what to do but also how to do it. They distinguished goals from procedures and ends from means. Such means-end differentiation is a prerequisite to effective planning, for only with such ability can alternative means or plans be considered. The activities mentioned are listed in Table 2. Eleven other activities were mentioned once. Younger children noted plans for how to distract a baseball team, hurt someone, make a park, put a machine together,

Table 1. Frequencies of Specific Planning Goals

Plan	Times Mentioned	Younger	Older
1. What to do for your day/night	9	3	6
2. To go somewhere	8	4	4
3. To go home after school with a friend	6	4	2
4. To go on a trip	6	4	2
5. To have a surprise birthday party	5	4	1
6. To rob something	5	2	3
7. To write a story or a book	4	1	3
8. To tell a joke or do a trick	2	2	0
9. To get a job	2	0	2
10. To bring gym shorts to school	2	1	1
11. To move to a new house	2	1	1

teach someone to tie a shoe, and tease a brother. Older children referred to plans for answering interview questions, doing something (generic), reading a story, running football plays, and solving crimes. Overall, older children gave more method-planning responses than did younger children (twenty-two versus twelve), but they gave about the same number of different responses (twelve versus ten). Three response categories constituted most of the nineteen examples. Building activities (numbers 1 and 3) were the focus of twelve of thirty-four responses, activity scheduling (numbers 2 and 4) was mentioned for five of thirty-four responses, and game strategies (numbers 6 and 8) were the examples given for six of thirty-four responses. Method-planning for school activities (number 5) was generally neglected, with plans for how to study or do homework being mentioned only by older children.

Planning the Specific Conditions of Doing Something. Some children went beyond examples of planning to do something (at all) and beyond the generic-planning "how to do something" responses; they specified conditions of the plan. Such conditions constitute constraints, which further define the goal state to be achieved. Details of the plan were specified in terms of component acts, times and places for acts, and instruments required. The children noting

Table 2. Frequencies of Specific "How-to" Plans

Plan	Times Mentioned	Younger	Older
1. How to make or build something	7	2	5
2. How to do things in a certain order	4	0	4
3. How to build a building	3	0	3
4. How to arrange a schedule or a calendar	2	0	2
5. How to study for a test or do homework	2	0	2
6. How to play a game	2	2	0
7. How to solve something	2	1	1
8. How to put people in game positions	2	1	1

these constraints revealed a reflective awareness of the levels-of-abstraction dimension intrinsic to cognitive models of planning. We have distinguished four general classes of such responses: planning to do something at a certain time, planning to do something at a certain place, planning to do something with certain instruments, and planning the specific details of what to do in terms of a goal.

Planning to do something at a certain time. Eleven of the thirteen older children (but only 5 of the thirteen younger ones) mentioned time specifications for plans; eight older children (versus three younger children) gave the school-related example of setting a time to do homework or study for a test (see Table 3).

Planning to do something at a certain place. Children gave three examples: plans for where to stay during a trip (younger child), where to meet a person (one younger child, two older children), and where to meet to eat (older child).

Planning to do something with certain things. The only examples mentioned were planning what things are needed for a camping trip (younger child) or a vacation (older child).

Planning specific actions, given a prior goal choice. These are cases in which, once a decision has been made to do something (goal), greater goals specification becomes the aim of the plan. Two younger children each gave an example: planning what to buy while shopping, and planning how to celebrate a birthday. Two other examples were mentioned by older children: planning what to write for grammar class, and planning what to wear to school.

Prototypic Planners: Who Plans a Lot?

Asking children to talk about who plans a lot was another way to discover which activities children believe need planning. We reasoned that, from children's perspectives, people who frequently plan may serve as model planners, from whom children might learn how to better their own planning (see Table 4). Twenty other responses were contributed by different children. Younger children's examples included actors, company presidents, conductors, interviewers, managers, "my friends," robbers, and travelers. Older

Table 3. Frequencies of Time-Specific Plans

Plan	Times Mentioned	Younger	Older
1. When to do homework or study for a test	11	3	8
2. What time to go to school	3	1	2
3. When to do pet chores (feed cat, walk dog, clean bird cage)	2	0	2
4. When to go on dates	1	1	0
5. To wake up at a certain time	1	1	0
6. To schedule a time for class computer use	1	1	0
7. To meet friends at a certain time	1	0	1

Table 4. Frequencies of Specific Roles of Planners

Plan	Times Mentioned	Younger	Older
1. The President of the United States	8	3	5
2. Business people	8	3	5
3. Teachers	7	2	5
4. My family	3	2	1
5. Doctors/surgeons	3	0	3
6. Politicians	2	0	2
7. Architects	2	0	2
8. Rich people	2	1	1
9. Me	2	1	1
10. Everybody	2	1	1
11. Airline workers	2	1	1

children mentioned the Avon Lady, bakers and chefs, dentists, directors, garbage collectors, "important people," movie-star agents, "people with personality," producers, quarterbacks, scientists, and writers.

Reasons given for why these people plan a lot were generally that they have many actions to decide upon or to schedule. Less often, children noted the negative consequences that would occur if such planners did not plan: airplanes would crash, bakers would burn food, politicians would not get elected, robbers would get caught, and travelers would not go anywhere.

To Plan or Not to Plan?

It is crucial to understand the child's choice to plan or to proceed without explicit efforts at planning. With practice, one can attain a rich understanding of problems that arise in a content domain (such as in physics, for example; see Chi, Feltovich, and Glaser, 1981), so that adequate and efficient algorithms are available for solving problems and abrogate the need for explicit plan construction.

Are school-aged children reflectively aware of this distinction between "ritual" and "creative" plans? We approached this question by asking children to tell us about when and why they do not have to plan. Their answers can be categorized in terms of three major classes.

"You Don't Plan to Do Something You Are Just About to Do." These responses define nonplanning occasions as those when the activity will take place in the near future: "When it comes up, you just do the thing, you don't plan to do it" (five younger, three older).

"You Don't Plan to Do Something If Others Plan It for You." Here, children are noticing that if others (such as parents or teachers) plan for them they do not need to plan. The four older children who used this definition stated it generally: "When others plan for you"; only one of two younger children who used it did so. The other child gave specific examples: "When mom says, 'Go outside,' I don't plan to go outside, I just do."

"You Don't Plan If You Already Know What to Do." Children expressing this idea revealed that they distinguished creative from ritual plans. They designated only the former as genuine plans: "If you know already, if it's an everyday thing, you just do what you usually do." Five older and two younger children gave generic responses, whereas six older and three younger children offered specific examples: "You don't plan to read the word 'the'," and "You just go to sleep, you don't plan to."

Consequences of Not Planning

What motivates children to plan? We expect that children are inclined to plan when necessary, if they are aware of the consequences of not planning, such as potential nonachievement of their goals. When asked, "When you have to plan ahead, what would happen if you didn't?", almost all children said that the activity just would not work out if it were not planned. Instances of non-planning by these children are therefore unlikely to derive from ignorance of the potential negative consequences of not planning. Rather, the children appear to have different conceptions of which goal-directed behaviors require planning for successful performance.

Distinguishing "Better" From "Worse" Plans and Planners

How did children distinguish "better" from "worse" plans? Three major classes of responses were discerned (see Table 5). Most younger children appear to have a magical theory of plans: one will succeed with a good plan, but not otherwise. In this belief, they are different from the older children, who were more likely to view "better" plans as facilitators, but not guarantors, of goal achievement or as plans that allow alternative routes to goals as new circumstances arise. This last group of respondents recognized the tentative nature of plans and the revisionary nature of the planning process. Several other children offered responses based on four idiosyncratic criteria: *effort* ("Plans that are thought about more are better than those that are thought about less"); *trust* ("Plans that my friends, parents, and teachers tell me about are better than those I hear from other people"); *affect* ("Plans I like are better

Table 5. Concepts of "Better" and "Worse" Plans

Responses	*Times Mentioned*	*Younger*	*Older*
1. Better plans succeed; worse ones fail.	10	9	1
2. Better plans facilitate goal getting; worse ones do not.	6	0	6
3. Better plans are flexible, have several ways to work, and hence are well-adapted to their circumstances; worse plans have only one way to work.	3	1	2

than those I don't like"); and *morality* ("Plans that do good things are better than plans that do bad things").

In probing children's beliefs about what distinguishes "better" from "worse" planners, we found a wide range of responses (see Table 6). As we indicated earlier, planners need to believe that time and effort expended in planning will be rewarded by benefits from plan outcomes. It is therefore interesting that children believed effective planning to be time-intensive (numbers 3 and 5).

How Planning Works

Few children said anything about the specific elements of plan construction. Ericcson and Simon (1980) note that retrospection is reconstructive, in contrast with think-aloud reports during problem solving itself (which serve as "readouts" of working memory). It is possible that the difficulty of planning-process retrospection for these children arises from the demands of reconstructing a general process of planning from specific previous cases. Reconstruction would require a classifying of the similarities among all occasions of employing particular planning processes, as well as a self-reflective component-process analysis of planning activities. It is unlikely that children would remember their previous planning experiences or the similarities among them in such detail. In our current research, we ask children to think aloud while solving a planning problem that involves the integration of multiple goals. This method appears more promising as a key to revealing the organization of children's planning processes (Pea, Jewson, and Sheingold, forthcoming).

Three older children who referred to general features of planning processes said that they put the component actions of their plans in sequence: "I make up a schedule in my mind of what to do, in order"; "I make an order for

Table 6. Concepts of "Better and "Worse" Planners

Responses	Times Mentioned	Younger	Older
1. Better planners have more planning experience. that worse planners do.	8	3	5
2. There is no difference between them.	7	5	2
3. Better planners are patient and think for a long time; worse planners are in a hurry.	6	3	3
4. There is a difference but I can't say why.	5	2	3
5. Better planners start planning earlier than worse planners do.	2	1	1
6. Better planners make plans well adapted to circumstances.	1	0	1
7. Better planners make their plans in more detail.	1	0	1
8. Better planners are smarter.	1	1	0

what I'd rather do first, second, and third." Although some children mentioned a sequence for plan-component actions, none of them noted either the contingencies that may arise in plan execution and prompt plan revision or the other key features of planning processes. Only the second statement (above) reveals reflection of the role of goal priorities in the ordering of plan-component actions, yet goal priorities are an essential aspect of the principle of goal-value maximization, as discussed previously.

The Relative Difficulty of Planning Activities, and Factors Distinguishing "Easy Planning" from "Hard Planning"

All children felt that planning is sometimes hard and sometimes easy, but very few children mentioned identical factors as affecting the difficulty of planning activities. Planning was said to be harder if:

1. Component-act decisions are difficult: "It's hard if tough decisions have to be made on what to do."
2. Planning effort is great: "It's hard if you have to think really hard."
3. Plan size is large: "When you have more things to plan, it makes it harder to think and takes longer; it's easier with fewer things."
4. Plan revision is required: "It's harder when what's planned has to be changed."
5. Plans are not familiar: "It's easy if you know it, because you've done it before, but it's harder doing it for the first time."
6. Plans fail: "It's hard if the plan keeps on not happening."
7. Plan subject is disliked: "It's hard to plan if you don't like to think about it, as in math."
8. Efficient plan execution is desired: "It's easier to make it not work well, but harder if I want it to be better."
9. Planning context is noisy: "It's easier to plan when it is quiet than when it's noisy."
10. Plan execution is rapid: "If I have to do it in a rush, it's harder to do my best."
11. Plan is hard to remember: "It's easier if I write the plan down so that I can remember it, and check it off as I go along."
12. Plan domain is hard: "Whether it's easy or hard depends on what the plan's about."

Each child who mentioned a factor at all was unlikely to suggest any other features differentiating hard from easy planning. Collectively, this list is impressive, and reveals considerable sophistication and wisdom in children's thoughts about planning obstacles. Nevertheless, children seemed to respond with only a single difficulty factor, no matter how extensively they were questioned. The size of the plan (3), practice with the plan (5), attitude (7) and knowledge (12) regarding the planning topic, the effects of noise (9), selecting plan outcomes (1), and the need for greater effectiveness (8) are distinguished as factors that can make plan construction hard. Time constraints (10), plan "readability" (11), plan failure (6), and the need for revisions (4) are marked as factors that make plan execution hard.

Making Planning Easier

Planning can be difficult, and a major feature of planners who are consciously developing their planning skills is knowing how to seek help. This help may be either self-centered (relying on written lists, physical props as reminders, and so on) or other centered (another person may take over the planning entirely or planners may ask for hints, assistance in revising plans, or collaboration on plan construction and execution). We asked children how they make planning easier, and their responses included ways of improving both plan construction and "readability."

Self-Centered Planning Aids. Relatively few of the suggestions for making planning easier had to do with children's own activities. There were aids mentioned for plan formulation and "readability" (see Table 7).

Suggested aids for enhancing the "readability" of a plan for execution are shown in Table 8.

Other-Centered Planning Aids. By contrast, children talked a lot about ways that plan construction and execution could be made easier by others. Titles are listed in Tables 9 and 10 to match the role the other serves.

Discussion

These results show that school-aged children have fairly elaborate views of those activities they consider appropriate to planning, as well as of the consequences of not planning, the factors influencing planning difficulties, and the ways of aiding planning. Few children noted the flexible and revisionary nature of those planning processes that characterize advanced planning

Table 7. Aids to Plan Formulation

Responses	Times Mentioned	Younger	Older
1. Think about the plan more.	6	2	4
2. Do fewer things in the plan.	2	2	0
3. Use tricks, as in math.	1	0	1
4. Start planning earlier.	1	0	1

Table 8. Aids to Plan "Readability"

Responses	Times Mentioned	Younger	Older
1. Write the plan down.	4	1	3
2. Have a good memory for plans.	1	0	1

Table 9. Aids to Plan Construction

	Title	Description	Times Mentioned	Younger	Older
1.	Tutor	Gives suggestions or ideas for my plan.	16	7	9
2.	Reviser	Helps fix up or improve parts of my plan.	5	2	3
3.	Collaborator	Does part of the planning, while I do the other part.	4	2	2
4.	Planner	Makes the plan for me.	2	1	1
5.	Guide	Tells me whom to ask for help or what to read.	1	0	1
6.	Psychiatrist	Calms me down while I am planning.	1	0	1

Table 10. Aids to Plan Execution

	Title	Description	Times Mentioned	Younger	Older
1.	Mnemonic	Reminds me to carry out the plan.	2	1	1
2.	Coexecutor	Carries out part of the plan.	2	1	1

activities. Metaplanning principles—so central to the revisionary character of goal definition, plan construction, and plan execution—were mentioned by only a few children, who revealed their use of goal priorities in scheduling multiple activities. It is very striking that the problem-solving settings of schoolwork were virtually absent from children's accounts of planning occasions.

New Research Directions

Great interest in planning has accompanied the recent recognition of metacognition as an integral aspect of higher mental functioning (for example, Brown and DeLoache, 1978; Flavell, 1977). Soviet psychological theorists have also recognized that planning activity is fundamental to the organizational dynamics of psychological activity (Leont'ev, 1980). Attention to planning development has been confined, however, to age differences in the quantitative measures of planning, such as more moves mentioned (Klahr and Robinson, 1981) and "increasingly conscious control and regulation of goal-oriented strategies" (Brown and DeLoache, 1978). Studies influenced by Vygotsky's (1978) conception of the progressive internalization of cognitive processes have also been limited to more-less comparisons; the tutor "scaffolds" by verbalizing goals and component aspects of plans, and the child progressively takes over, or internalizes, parts of the planning activity (Gearhart and Newman, 1980; Wertsch and others, 1980).

While recognizing the social embeddedness of planning development, we have chosen here to emphasize those qualitative aspects of plan organization for an individual (in terms of structure and process) that are subject to developmental analysis (in the sense of development toward an ideal), as well as to progressive and regressive changes that may (but need not) be predictable from the passage of time. These analytical considerations are complementary to Vygotskian studies, which are directed toward elucidating social processes of planning ontogenesis, and they may illuminate the way we investigate such processes.

Most of this chapter has been a critical-developmental synthesis of the recent planning literature as it illuminates what planning development is the development of. Future research could reveal specific interrelationships among the various fronts on which planning activities may develop, as well as encouraging a deeper, process-oriented understanding of social and individual conditions that can help or hinder the development of planning abilities. Knowledge of developmental processes could also be integrated into school curricula and adult-education programs that are devoted to promoting planning development.

Since the extent and organization of knowledge in any problem-solving domain plays such a central role in simulating tentative plans and in revising plans during their execution, planning skills will need to be studied, as well as taught, in relation to specific contents. There are serious problems of nontransfer to other domains, and they are troublesome to proponents of planning and problem-solving skills (Tuma and Reif, 1980; Urbain and Kendall, 1980), but we believe that these problems can be alleviated if, for whatever domain is utilized, a major instructional aim is to convey a developmental perspective on planning and thereby connect the workings of common, formal properties of planning (particularly metaplanning principles) to the workings of more familiar domains. Novice problem-solvers may not spontaneously recognize the commonalities among planning processes across content domains.

We take two approaches to this problem in our current work. A common belief, unsupported by research, is that the development of computer-programming expertise promotes problem solving and planning activities in general (Papert, 1980), so that the transfer of revision and problem-decomposition skills is to be expected. We are investigating the development of one group of children's expertise in planning to solve computer-programming problems (that is, domain-specific planning). We have also been videotaping sessions of think-aloud planning for carrying out a list of classroom chores, with the same children, as well as others and some adults for comparison. The chore-scheduling task was designed on the basis of ethnographic work, to ensure that all the children carried out such chores regularly. Presumably, then, there are no differences between the groups of children in terms of planning-domain knowledge, but, rather, only in their use of planning abilities.

This reserach enables us to examine microgenetic processes (Flavell and Draguns, 1957) as children proceed through a developmental sequence of multiple plan formulations toward their best (shortest distance) plans. Our goal is to determine whether any developmental gains in planning skills that may have been achieved through programming experience will be demonstrated anew in the chore-scheduling task. The qualitative aspects of plan structure and planning processes that we have outlined will be the main focus of our analyses.

References

Anzai, Y., and Simon, H. "The Theory of Learning by Doing." *Psychological Review,* 1979, *86,* 124-140.
Baker, L., and Brown, A. L. "Metacognitive Skills of Reading." In D. Pearson (Ed.), *Handbook of Reading Research.* New York: Longman, 1980.
Brown, A. L., and DeLoache, J. S. "Skills, Plans, and Self-Regulation." In R. S. Siegler (Ed.), *Children's Thinking: What Develops?* Hillsdale, N.J.: Erlbaum, 1978.
Bruce, B., and Newman, D. "Interacting Plans." *Cognitive Science,* 1978, *2,* 195-233.
Bullock, M., Gelman, R., and Baillargeon, R. "The Development of Causal Reasoning." In W. Friedman (Ed.), *The Developmental Psychology of Time.* New York: Academic Press, in press.
Burke, K. *A Grammar of Motives.* New York: Prentice-Hall, 1945.
Byrne, R. "Planning Meals: Problem-Solving on a Real Data-Base." *Cognition,* 1977, *5,* 287-332.
Case, R. "Intellectual Development from Birth to Adulthood: A Neo-Piagetian Interpretation." In R. S. Siegler (Ed.), *Children's Thinking: What Develops?* Hillsdale, N.J.: Erlbaum, 1978.
Chi, M. T. H., Feltovich, P. J., and Glaser, R. "Categorization and Representation of Physics Problems by Experts and Novices." *Cognitive Science,* 1981, *5,* 121-152.
Dewey, J. *Human Nature and Conduct.* New York: Henry Holt, 1922.
Ericcson, K. A., and Simon, H. "Verbal Reports as Data." *Psychological Review,* 1980, *87,* 215-251.
Ernst, G. W., and Newell, A. *GPS: A Case Study in Generality and Problem Solving.* New York: Academic Press, 1969.
Fikes, R. E., and Nilsson, N.J. "STRIPS: A New Approach to the Application of Theorem Proving to Problem Solving." *Artificial Intelligence,* 1971, *2,* 189-203.
Flavell, J. H. *Cognitive Development.* Englewood Cliffs, N.J.: Prentice-Hall, 1977.
Flavell, J., and Draguns, J. "A Microgenetic Approach to Perception and Thought." *Psychological Bulletin,* 1957, *54,* 197-217.
Gearhart, M., and Newman, D. "Learning to Draw a Picture: The Social Context of an Individual Activity." *Discourse Processes,* 1980, *3,* 160-184.
Goldin, S. E., and Hayes-Roth, B. *Individual Differences in Planning Processes.* A Rand Note (N-1488-ONR), September 1980.
Hayes-Roth, B. *Estimation of Time Requirements During Planning: The Interactions Between Motivation and Cognition.* A Rand Note (N-1581-ONR), November 1980.
Hayes-Roth, B., and Hayes-Roth, F. "A Cognitive Model of Planning." *Cognitive Science,* 1979, *3,* 275-310.
Jeffries, R., Turner, A. A., Polson, P. G., and Atwood, M. E. "The Processes Involved in Designing Software." In J. R. Anderson (Ed.), *Cognitive Skills and Their Acquisition.* Hillsdale, N.J.: Erlbaum, 1981.
Kaplan, B. "Meditations on Genesis." *Human Development,* 1967, *10,* 65-87.
Kaplan, B. "Genetic-Dramatism." In S. Wapner and B. Kaplan (Eds.), *Toward a Holistic Developmental Psychology.* Hillsdale, N.J.: Erlbaum, 1982.
Klahr, D., and Robinson, M. "Formal Assessment of Problem-Solving and Planning Processes in Preschool Children." *Cognitive Psychology,* 1981, *13,* 113-147.

Kotarbinski, T. (Trans. O. Wojtasiewicz). *Praxiology: An Introduction to the Sciences of Efficient Action.* Oxford: Pergamon Press, 1965.

Kreutzer, M.A., Leonard, C., and Flavell, J. H. "An Interview Study of Children's Knowledge About Memory." *Monographs of the Society for Research in Child Development,* 1975, *40* (1), Serial no. 159.

Leont'ev, A. M. "The Problem of Activity in Psychology." In J. V. Wertsch (Ed.), *The Concept of Activity in Soviet Psychology.* Armonk, N.Y.: Sharpe Press, 1980.

Levy, F. K., Thompson, G. L., and Wiest, J. D. "The ABC's of the Critical Path Method." *Harvard Business Review,* 1963, *41,* 98–108.

Meacham, J. A., and Kushner, S. "Anxiety, Prospective Remembering, and the Performance of Planned Actions." *Journal of General Psychology,* in press.

Miller, G. A., Galanter, E., and Pribram, K. H. *Plans and the Structure of Behavior.* New York: Holt, Rinehart and Winston, 1960.

Nelson, K., and Gruendel, J. M. "At Morning It's Lunchtime: A Scriptal View of Children's Dialogues." *Discourse Processes,* 1979, *2,* 73–94.

Newell, A., and Simon, H. *Human Problem Solving.* Englewood Cliffs, N.J.: Prentice-Hall, 1972.

Papert, S. *Mindstorms.* New York: Basic Books, 1980.

Pea, R. D., Jewson, J., and Sheingold, K. "Microgenetic Developmental Analyses of Planning Processes in a Chore-Scheduling Task." In S. Friedman, E. Scholnick, and R. Cocking (Eds.), *The Development of Cognitive and Social Planning Behavior,* forthcoming.

Polya, G. *How to Solve It.* New York: Doubleday, 1945.

Sacerdoti, E. D. *A Structure for Plans and Behavior.* North-Holland, Amsterdam: Elsevier, 1977.

Schank, R. C., and Abelson, R. P. *Scripts, Plans, Goals, and Understanding.* Hillsdale, N.J.: Erlbaum, 1977.

Schutz, A. "Choosing Among Projects of Action." In *Collected Papers.* Vol. I: *The Problem of Social Reality.* The Hague, Netherlands: Martinus Nijhoff, 1973.

Siegler, R. S. "Developmental Sequences Within and Between Concepts." *Monographs of the Society for Research in Child Development,* 1981, *56* (2), entire volume.

Stefik, M. "Planning and Metaplanning (MOLGEN: Part 2)." *Artifical Intelligence,* 1981a, *16,* 141–170.

Stefik, M. "Planning with Constraints (MOLGEN: Part 2)." *Artificial Intellegnece,* 1981b, *16,* 111–140.

Thorndyke, P. W. "Pattern-Directed Processing of Knowledge from Text." In D. A. Waterman and F. Hayes-Roth (Eds.), *Pattern-Directed Inference Systems.* New York: Academic Press, 1978.

Tuma, D. T., and Reif, F. (Eds.). *Problem Solving and Education: Issues in Teaching and Research.* Hillsdale, N.J.: Erlbaum, 1980.

Urbain, E. S., and Kendall, P.C. "Review of Social-Cognitive Problem-Solving Interventions with Children." *Psychological Bulletin,* 1980, *88,* 109–143.

Vygotsky, L. S. *Mind in Society: The Development of Higher Psychological Processes.* Cambridge, Mass.: Harvard University Press, 1978.

Wapner, S., and Cirillo, L. "Development and Individual Differences in Planning." PHS grant proposal, Department of Psychology, Clark University, 1974.

Werner, H. "The Concept of Development from a Comparative and Organismic Point of View." In D. R. Harris (Ed.), *The Concept of Development.* Minneapolis: University of Minnesota Press, 1957.

Wertsch, J., Dowley McNamee, G., McLane, J. B., and Budwig, N. A. "The Adult-Child Dyad as a Problem-Solving System." *Child Development,* 1980, *51,* 1215–1221.

Wilensky, R. "Meta-Planning: Representing and Using Knowledge About Planning in Problem Solving and Natural Language Understanding." *Cognitive Science,* 1981, *5,* 197–233.

Roy D. Pea is research psychologist at the Bank Street College of Education's Center for Children and Technology and research assistant professor at the Heinz Werner Institute for Developmental Psychology, Clark University.

A review of the literature on children's referential communication ability suggests how these studies help us understand children's planning in their social interactions with others.

Planning and the Development of Communication Skills

Charlotte J. Patterson
Ralph J. Roberts, Jr.

Although many kinds of everyday communication seem to require relatively little forethought on the part of participants, there are certainly cases in which extensive planning is necessary for success. Consider, for example, the academic job interview: Before going to the interview, the candidate generally prepares an oral presentation of his or her recent research. Taking into account both the nature of the material to be presented and the expected nature of the audience, the candidate decides what should be highlighted and what should be passed over quickly and then organizes the talk accordingly, selecting appropriate visual aids and often even rehearsing in front of friendly colleagues. Only after such preparations have been completed does the candidate actually go to the interview. Those who must evaluate the candidate also think about the kinds of inquiries they will make. Clearly, a great deal of conscious effort goes into planning this kind of communication.

While we are all aware that adults plan certain kinds of communication extensively, we know much less about the extent to which children plan communicative episodes or about how their ability to do so develops with age. In recent years, there has been considerable interest in the development of children's planfulness with reference to memorization and other cognitive tasks (see, for example, Brown and DeLoache, 1978; Flavell, 1977, 1981; Flavell and Wellman, 1977; Pea, this volume). With some exceptions (for example, Cosgrove and Patterson, 1977, 1978; Schmidt and Paris, 1982), however, there has been relatively little attention to the development of planning as it relates to referential communication skills acquired during childhood.

In this chapter, we shall focus mainly on children's referential communication and shall be concerned principally with the kinds of skills that may be necessary for successful planning of referential communication. Performance on referential-communication tasks has been related to indices of social competence (Gottman, Gonso, and Rasmussen, 1975), as well as to academic achievement (Patterson and Kister, 1981). Thus, the extensive research literature on the development of children's referential-communication skills (for reviews, see Asher, 1979; Glucksberg, Krauss, and Higgins, 1975; Patterson and Kister, 1981) provides a good data-base for examining the component skills necessary for planning in at least one significant communication context.

After surveying the available information on referential communication, we shall offer some conclusions about the development of planning processes in this domain and consider briefly some possible implications of our conclusions for the planning of other, more complex, communicative activities. To accomplish these things, however, we must first consider the concept of planning itself (compare Miller, Galanter, and Pribram, 1960).

What are the chief characteristics of planning activities? First, plans are constructed to effect some change: We develop plans to change some current state—the status quo—into some other desired state—the goal state; thus, plans are goal-oriented. The job candidate preparing a colloquium, for example, has a major goal of informing the audience about the most interesting and novel aspects of his or her research, and the planning of the colloquium will be oriented toward this goal. Second, planning involves selection of both content and order of the activities that will be undertaken to achieve the goal. Such planning may be either very specific and detailed or quite general and flexible. For example, the job candidate's planning might extend to a fully written-out version of the colloquium, or it might be limited to a rough outline. In either case, however, the plan constrains and organizes both the content and the order of the actions to be performed. Third, planning involves hierarchical organization of goals and subgoals. The job candidate's general goal for the colloquium may be to inform the audience about important aspects of his or her research, but the audience's attention must also be held if this goal is to be achieved. Hence, a subgoal that the candidate must consider is to engage the audience and to generate interest in the material to be presented; this subgoal, however, must not overwhelm the information value of the finished talk. In other words, the plan must be hierarchically organized.

Fully elaborated plans must also include criteria for evaluating the activities performed under their direction, and such evaluation depends on a test of efficacy. In some cases, this is a straightforward and easily met requirement. In other cases, however, providing appropriate criteria may be more difficult.

At a minimum, then, planning involves the selection and hierarchical organization of goals and subgoals, selection of the content and the order of activities appropriate to achieve the goal(s), and the adoption of criteria against which planning efforts and their outcomes can be assessed. Thus, planning activities certainly require some amount of anticipation or knowledge, both of actions to be undertaken and conditions under which they will be performed, but the degree to which planning activities must be conscious is open to question. Activities such as planning a colloquium obviously involve substantial conscious effort, but other kinds of planning may be almost entirely automatic and require relatively little conscious effort or attention.

What kinds of skills and knowledge must children have mastered before they can carry out such planning activities for referential communication; and to what extent do children of different ages possess these skills? After we examine the literature for answers to these questions, we shall consider the implications these answers may have for children's ability to plan referential and other kinds of communication.

Components of Skill for Referential Communication

Much of the information available on the development of referential-communication skills has been gathered in the context of the paradigm developed by Glucksberg and Krauss (for example, Glucksberg, Krauss, and Higgins, 1975; Glucksberg, Krauss, and Weisberg, 1966). In this paradigm, one person (the speaker) is asked to describe a referent object or a picture so that, on the sole basis of the speaker's verbal message, another person (the listener) can select that target referent from a group of potential referents. In this situation, the speaker's goal is to produce a message that identifies the attribute or attributes distinguishing the target from other potential referents. Using the information provided in the speaker's message or messages, the listener's goal is to select the correct (target) referent from among the group of potential referents.

What kinds of component skills are required for a fully developed ability to plan referential-communication performances in this kind of setting? Depending on whether one will be performing in the speaker or in the listener role, somewhat different kinds of activities may be required. A speaker in referential communication is mainly concerned with transmission of information; a listener, with reception. Their respective activities need to be organized with these goals in mind (compare Higgins, Fondacaro, and McCann, 1981). Accordingly, we shall examine separately the literature on speaker roles and listener roles.

The component-skill categories identified below, while certainly not exhaustive, are intended to provide a framework for considering the development of communicative skill. The component-analysis approach seems particularly useful, in that it allows detailed descriptions of competencies as well as deficiencies at different developmental levels (compare Roberts, 1981). In addition, attention to component skills allows for identification of both the extent to which and the specific ways in which various task factors affect children's communicative performances.

Components of Speaker Skill

Before children can learn to make adequate plans for performances in the speaker role, they must have basic knowledge about the nature of referential communication itself. Children must also be able to identify and label principal features of stimuli and to select message contents. In some cases, children must also be able to order the elements of a message and repair communication breakdowns. We shall briefly examine the developmental literature relevant to each of these five kinds of component skills.

Basic Knowledge About the Speaker Role. Before children can communicate effectively, they must have attained a basic level of knowledge about the speaker role in referential communication. For example, the speaker must realize that, while he or she knows the identity of the target referent, the listener does not. While seemingly a simple achievement, this kind of understanding actually requires a rudimentary form of conceptual perspective-taking: It requires the ability to recognize that another person's state of knowledge differs from one's own (compare Glucksberg, Krauss, and Higgins, 1975; Marvin, Greenberg, and Mossler, 1976).

In a recent study (Roberts and Patterson, in press), we assessed this basic level of understanding among four- to six-year-olds in a referential-communication setting. Of the forty-two children tested, thirty-six (86 percent) gave evidence of this kind of understanding: These children indicated that, before any messages were communicated, they knew the identity of the target referent, but that their listeners did not. The six remaining children said that the listener knew the identity of the target referent before any messages were communicated. It appears, then, that some young children fail to grasp the basic premise of the speaker's efforts in referential communication, but most children demonstrate this understanding by four or five years of age.

Another important form of speaker knowledge is that the purpose of the message is to inform the listener. In the study just mentioned (Roberts and Patterson, in press) we found that, regardless of whether their messages were informative or not, children who appreciated the initial discrepancy between the speaker's and the listener's perspectives believed their messages were adequate to inform the listener. Thus, these basic understandings of the referential-communication situation seem necessary for optimal speaker performance, but they are not sufficient.

Identification of Relevant Stimulus Attributes. In most referential-communication situations, the target referent must be distinguished from a surrounding array of potential referents. The target and potential referents typically have some attributes in common, but differ with regard to others. The ability to identify features that distinguish the target from the potential referents is therefore crucial to producing informative messages.

In some cases, identification and labeling of the target referent's distinguishing features is a very simple task. For example, when the target and potential referents are pictures of different animals, even five-year-old speakers give adequate, informative messages (Glucksberg, Krauss, and Higgins, 1975; Glucksberg, Krauss, and Weisberg, 1966). When potential referents are very similar to one another, however, children may have difficulty making the necessary comparisons. For example, Vurpillot (1968) found that, when asked to determine whether two pictured houses were identical, four-year-olds often failed to examine both houses exhaustively before pronouncing them identical. They rarely made the necessary paired comparisons between relevant features of the houses that older (nine-year-old) children made. This finding is important because, to the extent that younger children fail to make the relevant comparisons among stimuli, they will also almost certainly fail to produce adequate messages on a regular basis as speakers.

Evidence consistent with this view of the role comparison skills play in developing referential-communication ability has been reported by Roberts and Patterson (in press). In this study, preschoolers' ability to distinguish the relevant differences between stimuli showed a significant negative correlation with the number of uninformative messages they produced, even after the contribution of chronological age had been partialed out.

Thus, the ability to identify differences among stimuli is a crucial component of speaker skill and often presents difficulties for younger children. Access to this component skill, however, does not guarantee its use. Before comparison skills can become useful to children in the speaker role, the need for their use in selecting message contents must be appreciated (compare Flavell, 1977; Roberts and Patterson, in press; Whitehurst and Sonnenschein, 1981).

Selecting Appropriate Message Contents. It has been documented repeatedly that younger children often fail to select appropriate message contents, producing instead uninformative messages that omit crucial information needed by the listener (compare Asher, 1979; Glucksberg, Krauss, and Higgins, 1975). What is the source of young children's difficulties in this respect? One possible answer (Asher, 1979; Asher and Oden, 1976) is that younger children often fail to make the relevant comparisons among stimuli and therefore fail to identify attributes that distinguish a target referent from distractors. As one might expect, on the basis of the literature just discussed, this hypothesis has received considerable support. Younger (for example, preschool) children often fail to compare referent and nonreferent before constructing a message (Asher and Oden, 1976); and, the more complicated and extensive the comparisons are, the less likely children are to complete the comparisons (Whitehurst, 1976; Whitehurst and Sonnenschein, 1978).

Why do young children fail to complete these comparison activities? As Whitehurst and Sonnenschein (1981) have argued, it may be that children do not know how to make the relevant comparisons or that they do not know when it is appropriate to do so. In a series of studies these authors showed that, although four- and five-year-olds were often able to complete comparisons among stimuli (and therefore to identify crucial attributes of the target referent), they often failed to do so in the speaker role (Whitehurst and Sonnenschein, 1981). In other words, even though these children knew how to do the appropriate thing, they did not know when to do it; they did not appear to realize that comparison activities were relevant to selecting appropriate message contents: "The young child does not know that to communicate referentially is to describe differences" (Whitehurst and Sonnenschein, 1981, p. 139).

Taking the inquiry one step further, we might also ask what factors account for this lack of knowledge. One possible answer to this question considers the child's perspective-taking skills. A speaker with good perspective-taking skills can see a situation from the listener's standpoint. Such a view provides an appropriate criterion for evaluating potential messages: an informative message describes differences between target and potential referents.

This perspective-taking hypothesis has been widely studied (compare Asher, 1979; Glucksberg, Krauss, and Higgins, 1975; Shantz, 1981), but most of the studies providing separate measures of perspective taking and referential communication have assessed these skills in different contexts, with different materials, and with widely varying task demands. Therefore, it is, perhaps, not surprising that there has been scant evidence for this hypothesis (Asher, 1979; Glucksberg, Krauss, and Higgins, 1975; Shantz, 1981).

More recently, however, Roberts and Patterson (in press) examined children's perspective-taking skills within a communication context, as well as assessing the relation of this skill to speaker performance in referential communication. In this study, preschool children were tested on each of three tasks: a referential-communication task that assessed speaker performance, a perspective-evaluation task that assessed the speaker's understanding of the listener's informational needs, and a comparison task that assessed the ability to isolate crucial attributes of the stimuli used in the other two tasks.

As expected, on the basis of earlier findings (for example, Whitehurst and Sonnenschein, 1981), results showed that, although most children were able to identify the crucial attributes of stimuli in the comparison task, they often failed to mention these attributes in their messages. Of more central interest here, however, was the finding that performance on the perspective-evaluation task showed a strong positive relationship to speaker performance, independent of the effects of age, task ordering, and performance on the comparison task. Perspective-taking skill, when assessed within a communication setting, emerged as systematically related to referential-communication skill.

In considering these results, it is notable that the children's messages on the referential-communication task were consistent with their own criteria for information necessary to inform the listener. Children who understood the listener's informational requirements (as assessed by the perspective-evaluation task) realized that only messages distinguishing the referent from potential referents would inform the listener. Children who did not fully appreciate the listener's perspective believed that a message needed only to describe (not necessarily distinguish) the target referent. The results of this study suggest the importance of perspective-taking skill in the speaker's adoption of criteria for selecting messages that will inform a listener.

To summarize, inability to make relevant comparisons among stimuli certainly limits a speaker's ability to produce informative messages. Beyond this, however, children capable of completing relevant comparisons do not always do so when constructing messages; they do not seem to regard comparison activities as relevant, because they lack the perspective-taking skill required to assess the listener's informational requirements. In our reading of the literature, perspective-taking and comparison skills both emerge as important skill components of selecting appropriate message contents.

Ordering Elements of the Message. Apart from selecting the contents of a message, another important speaker-role skill is the ability to order elements of the message effectively. Since many of the referential tasks that have been widely investigated do not call for ordering skills, they have received relatively little research attention to date.

Pratt, Scribner, and Cole (1977) asked children to explain to another child how to play a game. Older children typically began their explanations with descriptions of the game materials (thus orienting their listeners immediately to this essential information), but preschool children inserted these descriptions only haphazardly, sometimes in the middle and sometimes at the end of their explanations; the preschoolers did not seem to organize the contents of their explanations in a fashion that would enhance understanding. Little else seems to be known about development of the ability to order message contents or about how this ability contributes in general to effectiveness in the speaker role.

Repairing Communication Breakdowns. Another important speaker-role skill is the ability to monitor success and failure of communication efforts and repair communication breakdowns. In this regard, an effective speaker might be expected to monitor the listener's likely state of knowledge after receiving a message, request listener feedback about the message's adequacy, and respond to any feedback the listener offers by altering the message appropriately. Although there is relatively little information on children's performances of the first two kinds of activities (Roberts and Patterson, in press), there is a sizable literature on children's responses to listener feedback.

In general, the findings are as follows: Although they may not succeed in providing additional information, children as young as five years old usually make some attempt to respond when listeners request more information

(Cosgrove and Patterson, 1979; Karabenick and Miller, 1977). Under very simple and conducive task conditions, even four- and five-year-olds often succeed in improving their messages in response to listener feedback (Cosgrove and Patterson, 1979; Peterson, Danner, and Flavell, 1972). Older children, however, are much more likely than younger ones to respond appropriately to listener feedback (Flavell and others, 1968; Peterson, Danner, and Flavell, 1972). In addition, the nature of the feedback itself makes a difference in the response: Listener feedback that identifies specific message deficiencies generally elicits better responses from children of all ages than does feedback that indicates noncomprehension in more global terms (Cosgrove and Patterson, 1979; Peterson, Danner, and Flavell, 1972).

Components of Listener Skill

Just as children must have gained command of a variety of skills before they can begin to plan effective performances in the speaker role, so also are a number of component skills relevant to performance in the listener role. Apart from the ability to identify relevant stimulus attributes (discussed above), other elements specifically relevant to listener performance have been identified (compare Patterson and Kister, 1981). Among these are posession of basic knowledge about the communication situation itself, ability to assess the quality of messages produced by the speaker, and ability to produce appropriate responses to speaker messages. We shall consider the developmental literature relevant to each of these listener-performance elements in turn.

Basic Knowledge About the Listener Role in Referential Communication. Beyond recognizing their own initial ignorance of the target referent's identity, listeners should also understand the role of the message—namely, to inform them. At the most basic level, young children appear to exhibit this understanding: When messages are informative, even four-year-olds use the information contained in them to choose the target referents (Cosgrove and Patterson, 1977; Glucksberg, Krauss, and Higgins, 1975; Ironsmith and Whitehurst, 1978) and, under these circumstances, they appear to appreciate the role of the message. Sometimes, however, listeners must respond to messages that are not informative. In terms of their information value, messages can be categorized as informative (referring uniquely to one target referent), ambiguous (referring to more than one potential referent), or inappropriate (not referring to any of the potential referents). Of course, degrees of ambiguity are also possible. Unless listeners understand that ambiguous and inappropriate messages can lead to communication failure, they will be unlikely to request clarification even in response to messages that have been judged inadequate. Indeed, a child who does not understand the role of the message in communication may not be motivated even to assess the message's adequacy. Knowledge about the role of the message is therefore particularly important when messages are ambiguous or inappropriate.

There is evidence suggesting that knowledge about the role of the message is either better-developed or more easily applied in the case of inappropriate, as compared to ambiguous, messages. For example, Robinson and Robinson (1977b) exposed six-year-olds to informative, ambiguous, and inappropriate messages. When communication failed, they asked the children to assign blame to either the speaker or the listener. Children who blamed the listener for communication failure when the message was ambiguous were the same ones who blamed the speaker when the message was inappropriate; communication problems produced by inappropriate messages were apparently recognized more easily than those caused by ambiguous messages.

Other evidence suggests that lack of knowledge about the role of the message may limit young children's effectiveness as listeners, especially when messages are ambiguous (for example, Beal and Flavell, 1982; Robinson, 1981). For example (Robinson and Robinson, 1978), five- to eight-year-old children who were able to identify ambiguities in a speaker's message still blamed the listener for communication failures. Although they were aware of message deficiencies, these children did not suggest improving the message as a way of facilitating the communication, nor could they support the idea that the speaker might deserve the blame for such communication failures. Thus, even though they may be able to identify (for example, Robinson and Robinson, 1978) and remember (for example, Beal and Flavell, 1982) crucial attributes of target and potential referents, young children still may fail to appreciate the role of the message in communcation.

One possible explanation for this failure has been suggested by Ackerman (1981). On the basis of distinctions offered by Austin (1962), Ackerman argued that young children may be focusing on performative rather than propositional interpretations of the referential-communication situation and, hence, that they may be responding primarily to performative demands (for example, to select a referent), rather than to propositional contents (for example, informational adequacy) of speakers' messages. In support of this argument, Ackerman showed that, when performative force was de-emphasized in the communication situation, even five-year-olds were able to respond to the propositional content of inadequate messages (for example, by labeling them as ambiguous). Recognizing the primacy of a message's propositional aspects is an important part of understanding the message's role in referential-communication settings, and young children's lack of such awareness may limit their performances in the listener role.

Assessing Message Adequacy. Another skill essential to listener-role performance is the ability to evaluate the adequacy of the speaker's messages. Until listeners can rely on this ability, little effective communication planning can be expected from them. To what extent, and in what circumstances, are children able to monitor message quality, and how do these skills develop with age?

Some investigators have reported successful message-quality assessment among young children. For example, Patterson and others (1981) found that, under conditions of low stimulus complexity and high message ambiguity, six-year-olds provided accurate assessments of message quality. More recently, Pratt and Bates (1982) found that, with the help of a supportive perceptual context, even four-year-olds were able to evaluate message adequacy. Nevertheless, other studies have yielded much higher age estimates for development of message-evaluation skills. For instance, in one of the earliest studies (Flavell and others, 1968), third, seventh, and eighth graders were asked to evaluate the adequacy of directions for getting from one spot on a map to another. Third graders were quite unsuccessful in this regard, reporting an average of only one in four of the ambiguities contained in the directions. Even eleventh graders were not completely successful, reporting fewer than 75 percent of the inadequacies.

Clearly, referential-communication tasks vary widely among themselves in terms of their difficulty and, therefore, also in terms of the ages at which they are likely to be mastered. To get a more precise picture of developmental changes in this domain, it may be helpful to consider some of the factors that influence task difficulty.

One such factor is the nature of the message to be evaluated. In general, the research shows that the degree of a message's inadequacy is an influential factor. For example, Patterson and others (1981) studied five-, seven-, and nine-year-old children in the listener role in a standard referential-communication situation. The speaker produced messages that were either adequate, somewhat ambiguous, or very ambiguous, and the children were asked whether the messages allowed them to select unique target referents. Although older children were generally more successful, almost all children identified adequate messages, and correct appraisal of inadequate messages was more likely when messages were very ambiguous. The general conclusion from these findings—that the difficulty of message-appraisal tasks is strongly affected by message quality—is also supported by a number of other findings in the literature (compare Asher, 1979; Flavell and others, 1981; Patterson and Kister, 1981).

Another factor that appears to affect message-appraisal performances, especially for younger children, is outcome of the communicative episode. For instance, Robinson and Robinson (1977a) reported that six- and seven-year-olds were more likely to judge an ambiguous message adequate when it led to communicative success (for example, by chance) than when it led to failure. Older children were far less likely to be misled by outcomes when judging message adequacy. Even when they are explicitly informed of message ambiguity, five-year-olds are still more likely to judge a message adequate when it leads to communicative success (Singer and Flavell, 1981). Still another factor influencing message appraisal is size and distinctness of the array of potential referents. For example, Pratt and Bates (1982) found that four-year-olds evaluated message adequacy with more success when potential referent objects were physically present in front of them than when these objects were absent. Studies employing quite simple, distinct, and salient arrays of potential referents (Bearison and Levey, 1977; Patterson and others, 1981; Pratt and Bates, 1982) have generally yielded relatively low age norms for successful performance of message-appraisal tasks. In contrast, studies employing more complex stimulus materials have generally yielded higher age norms (for example, Flavell and others, 1968; Markman, 1981).

Responses to Adequate and Inadequate Messages. When children have basic understanding of a referential-communication situation and have also distinguished adequate from inadequate messages, they still must provide appropriate responses. When messages are adequate, verbal responses can help communication by reducing redundancy and enhancing efficiency (see, for example, Dittman, 1972; Karabenick and Miller, 1977). Verbal responses are not mandatory when messages are informative, but they are vital to communicative success when messages are ambiguous or inappropriate.

When a message is inadequate, an effective listener should attempt to point out ambiguous or inappropriate aspects of the message and/or request more information. Even when the stimulus situation is quite simple, however, children often have difficulty providing these responses. For example, Cosgove and Patterson (1977) found that four-, six-, and eight-year-old listeners rarely responded to ambiguous messages by requesting clarification; in that study, only ten-year-olds showed any substantial spontaneous tendency to provide appropriate listener responses. Similar findings have been reported by others (compare Patterson and Kister, 1981). Young children often do not appear to think of asking questions as a suitable strategy for getting more information when a speaker's initial message is inadequate, and this, in turn, limits their communicative effectiveness.

Related findings indicate, however, that the ability to make appropriate listener responses is well within the repertoire of even a fairly young child (Cosgrove and Patterson, 1977; Patterson, Massad, and Cosgrove, 1978). For example, when children in the Cosgrove and Patterson (1977) study were given a simple plan for effective listening (namely, instructions that emphasized the importance of asking questions if the speaker's message was inadequate), the performances of six-, eight-, and ten-year-olds improved markedly. Subsequent research (Patterson, Massad, and Cosgrove, 1978) revealed that, for these children, the likely locus of effect for the plan was in specifying the content and the timing of appropriate listener responses. Considered together, the results of these and related studies suggest that knowing how to request additional information is an important listener skill, which children may possess relatively early, but which they learn only gradually to apply precisely in referential-communication settings (Patterson and Kister, 1981).

Summary. Our reading of the literature reveals that young children have a number of well-developed skills for referential communication. In the speaker role, most four- and five-year-olds have a relatively solid knowledge-base concerning fundamental characteristics of communicative situations. In addition, these children are generally able to identify the crucial attributes of target referents in relatively simple stimulus situations. Thus, when relevant comparisons are very easy or when comparisons are not required, four- and five-year-olds often select appropriate message contents. Furthermore, when listener feedback is relatively specific about deficiencies in an initial message, five-year-old speakers are able to provide appropriate message alterations. Even when listener feedback is nonspecific, these preschool children seem to know that some response is called for, and they generally do respond in some way.

The young child also has considerable competence in the listener role. In response to an adequate message, even four-year-olds use information contained in the message to select the correct referent. Preschoolers also recognize that, to be adequate, a message must at least describe the target referent accurately; they reject inappropriate messages. When the stimulus array is very simple, four- and five-year-olds are also able to recognize ambiguous messages as inadequate. With some instruction, six-year-olds are able to make appropriate responses to inadequate messages.

Nevertheless, young children also experience many difficulties in referential communication. When the necessary comparisons among potential referents are numerous or difficult to make, four- and five-year-olds often fail to complete comparisons. Even with possession of relevant comparison skills, these children do not always use them to select message contents. This failure to employ comparison skills is associated with (and may derive from) incomplete appreciation of the listener's needs. Four- and five-year-olds also appear to have difficulty in ordering the elements of a lengthy message so as to enhance its communicative effectiveness. In addition, they often provide uninformative responses to listener feedback, especially when the feedback is nonspecific.

Young children's performances in the listener role are also limited in a number of ways. In more complex task situations (for example, when stimulus arrays are large and complicated, or when messages are only partially inadequate), four- and five-year-olds are unlikely to appraise message quality accurately. As might be expected, then, five- and even six-year-old listeners generally provide inadequate feedback about message adequacy; in particular, younger children only rarely request more information in response to inadequate messages.

The picture of the young child as a communicator that emerges is one of substantial but limited skill. Although preschoolers demonstrate proficiency in some referential-communication situations, they also demonstrate limitations, when compared with older children. These limitations appear to be of two principal kinds. With age and experience, children eventually acquire component skills necessary for the competent performance of referential-communication tasks. As they are acquired, however, these skills are initially limited, both in their effectiveness and in their range of application (compare Shatz, 1978). Having acquired certain rudimentary skills, a child gradually learns to use them with greater facility. As component skills (such as comparison and perspective taking) improve, the child learns to apply them to a broader range of communication problems, as well as to coordinate their use within a single communicative-task setting. Thus, development in this domain involves not only the acquisition of component skills but also increasing sophistication in their use.

Conclusion and Directions for Further Research

The precision and control afforded by the standard referential-communication paradigm have allowed for the detailed investigation of those component skills necessary for effective communication. Findings from these studies have helped us specify the kinds of communications skills children must acquire to communicate effectively. While there has been scant research explicitly concerned with the role of planning in children's referential communication, the findings in this area do have clear implications for the kinds of skills needed for effective planning of referential communication. We shall discuss some of these implications here and then suggest directions for future research.

One implication of the research we have reviewed is that effective planning seems heavily dependent on the selection of task-appropriate goals, with goal selection, in turn, heavily dependent on children's understanding of task situations. For example, a speaker who believes that the listener already knows the identity of the target referent, even before any messages have been communicated, will no doubt have goals very different from those of a speaker who realizes that the task is to inform the listener (compare Roberts and Patterson, in press). Similarly, a listener who believes that performative, rather than propositional, contents of a speaker's message are primary will have goals different from those of a listener who recognizes the significance of the message's propositional aspects (compare Ackerman, 1981). As judged by adult standards, then, children cannot be expected to develop effective planning activity until they have selected goals appropriate to the tasks in which they are engaged (compare Pea, this volume).

Another implication we can make is that the success of planning efforts for referential communication seems to depend strongly on control of the component skills necessary for executing the plan. For example, the ability to anticipate precise informational needs of a listener is clearly a skill important to the planning of message content. Without this ability, planning is less likely to help young speakers' performances (compare Roberts and Patterson, in press). Similarly, the ability to make accurate appraisals of message adequacy is a skill that is crucial to effective listener performance (compare Patterson and others, 1981). To the extent that children do not yet control the skills necessary for implementing plans, their efforts at communications planning are likely to remain ineffectual.

A related implication that we can make from the research evidence concerns the extent to which supportive contexts can facilitate not only communicative-task performances themselves but also, perhaps, planning activities. It has been found repeatedly that contexts offering perceptual support (for example, Pratt and Bates, 1982), specific feedback (for example, Peterson, Danner, and Flavell, 1972), and/or hints and plans (for example, Cosgrove and Patterson, 1977) tend to foster communicative success, especially among younger children. Older children are more successful at communicating over a wider range of nonsupportive task contexts; younger children, however, who have less well-developed component skills, are much more easily overloaded or swamped by task complexity (compare Shatz, 1978). Thus, supportive task contexts that reduce the amount and the complexity of cognitive processing help performance and may also make children's planning activities easier.

The conception emerging from these findings is similar to Bruner's (1975) notion of "scaffolding" in mother–infant interaction: "Scaffolding refers to the mother's effort to limit, so to speak, those degrees of freedom in the task that the child is not able to control" (Bruner, 1975, p. 12). In other words, by structuring the task environment, the mother enables her child to communicate more effectively than might otherwise be possible. With development, such scaffolding becomes less and less necessary, and the child becomes capable of functioning more independently.

The concept of scaffolding seems especially significant in understanding children's attempts to plan communicative episodes. It may be, for example, that supportive task contexts serve these scaffolding functions by allowing children to exercise still-fragile skills and by freeing their attention for planning activities. In less supportive contexts, young children must often struggle just to get through a task and will accordingly have less energy for planning. As children begin to require less and less supportive scaffolding to perform tasks correctly, planning activities become increasingly possible.

In general, then, research on children's referential communication has emphasized several kinds of variables that seem relevant to the development of planning skill. Such factors as a child's general knowledge about the communicative situation, the child's control of component skills, and the support provided by the task environment should all contribute to the child's ability to plan effectively. Although there is substantial literature on children's problem solving in other social contexts (Urbain and Kendall, 1980), there has been practically no research on children's developing ability to plan referential-communication episodes. We believe that this lack suggests some directions for research and will now consider some of these.

Before an adult describes or explains something to another, he or she will often spend time preparing for the communication. We have offered the example of a job candidate planning a colloquium. In this kind of situation, an opportunity for planning can obviously be crucial; not many people can deliver successful presentations on a completely extemporaneous basis. It is interesting to note, however, that the typical referential-communication situation for children requires them to give essentially extemporaneous performances. As a result, we know very little about children's abilities at different ages to use opportunities for planning. One very straightforward research approach would be to allow children of different ages several minutes for planning their performances before they undertake communicative tasks and to compare their performances with performances of children who have no opportunity to plan. If the referential-communication tasks were relatively complex (for example, describing the workings of a game), several developmental differences might emerge. Over and above the main effects that age has on performance adequacy, we might expect older children to have better knowledge of how to use planning time constructively and, therefore, also to benefit more from planning opportunities than younger children would. These effects should be more pronounced in more complex tasks and more evident in the nature of planning activities and the quality of task performances.

We anticipate that several components of communicative skill would be related to the ability to use planning periods effectively. For example, effective planning seems to require some knowledge about the performances being planned. Similarly, perspective-taking skill seems to be an important aspect of children's ability to anticipate not only listener needs but also possible obstacles to effective communication.

Children's ability to use planning opportunities effectively would also be expected to vary as a function of the task context. Young children's planning activities might be especially aided by task contexts that provided either social or nonsocial supports for these activities—for example, hints about how to construct a good plan or information on the availability of relevant materials (compare Urbain and Kendall, 1980). It seems likely that young children's planning efforts would benefit much more from such "scaffolding" than would those of older children.

Another promising area for investigation concerns the ways in which planning helps communicators who must pursue multiple communicative goals simultaneously. Using the job-candidate example again, we note that the candidate would be likely to plan a colloqium with more than one kind of communicative goal in mind: Informational goals would be clearly important, but goals relevant to entertainment and courtesy would also have to be taken into account; planning would help ensure that the colloquium would simultaneously achieve multiple goals.

Additional developmental research might focus on how children of different ages learn to coordinate communicative activities in pursuit of multiple goals, and on how they learn to use planning activities in this process. The basic research approach we have just discussed could be modified to allow the study of these questions. Children could be given more than one goal to achieve in their communicative performances; for example, they might be asked not only to explain the workings of a game but also to persuade a listener that the game is fun to play.

Apart from the overall age differences in communicative skill and in the ability to use planning time effectively, developmental differences in the ability to coordinate multiple goals might also emerge. For example, younger children might be limited to a serial manner of pursuing different goals—first one, then another. Older children, in contrast, might be expected to have greater success in coordinating their activities (for example, hierarchically) so as to pursue all their goals simultaneously. The effects of planning activities at different ages might prove especially interesting in this regard.

The research literature on the development of referential communication has already provided a useful base of knowledge about several component skills and task factors that influence communicative performance. Research on the development of planning skills should take these findings into account. As anyone who has ever prepared a colloquium for a job interview knows, planning communicative episodes is often a demanding and difficult task; many of the requisite kinds of skills and knowledge seem to be acquired late and even in adulthood are not always fully mastered. Therefore, future research on this topic will also need to include older age ranges than have been widely studied until now.

References

Ackerman, B. P. "Performative Bias in Children's Interpretations of Ambiguous Referential Communication." *Child Development*, 1981, *52*, 1224–1230.

Asher, S. R. "Referential Communication." In G. J. Whitehurst and B. J. Zimmerman (Eds.), *The Functions of Language and Cognition*. New York: Academic Press, 1979.

Asher, S. R., and Oden, S. L. "Children's Failure to Communicate: An Assessment of Comparison and Egocentrism Explanations." *Developmental Psychology*, 1976, *12*, 132–139.

Austin, J. L. *How to Do Things with Words*. London: Oxford University Press, 1962.

Beal, C. R., and Flavell, J. H. "Effect of Increasing the Salience of Message Ambiguities on Kindergartners' Evaluations of Communicative Success and Message Adequacy." *Developmental Psychology*, 1982, *18*, 43–48.

Bearison, D. J., and Levey, L. M. "Children's Comprehension of Referential Communication: Decoding Ambiguous Messages." *Child Development*, 1977, *48*, 716–720.

Brown, A. L., and DeLoache, J. S. "Skills, Plans, and Self-Regulation." In R. S. Siegler (Ed.), *Children's Thinking: What Develops?* Hillsdale, N.J.: Erlbaum, 1978.

Bruner, J. S. "The Ontogenesis of Speech Acts." *Journal of Child Language*, 1975, *2*, 1–19.

Cosgrove, J. M., and Patterson, C. J. "Plans and the Development of Listener Skills." *Developmental Psychology*, 1977, *13*, 357–564.

Cosgrove, J. M., and Patterson, C. J. "Generalization of Training for Children's Listener Skills." *Child Development*, 1978, *49*, 513–516.

Cosgrove, J. M., and Patterson, C. J. "Adequacy of Young Speakers' Encoding in Response to Listener Feedback." *Psychological Reports*, 1979, *45*, 15–18.

Dittman, A. T. "Developmental Factors in Conversational Behavior." *The Journal of Communication*, 1972, *22*, 404–423.

Flavell, J. H. *Cognitive Development*. Englewood Cliffs, N.J.: Prentice-Hall, 1977.

Flavell, J. H. "Cognitive Monitoring." In W. P. Dickson (Ed.), *Children's Oral Communication Skills*. New York: Academic Press, 1981.

Flavell, J. H., Botkin, P. T., Fry, C. L., Wright, J. C., and Jarvis, P. E. *The Development of Role-Taking and Communication Skills in Children*. New York: Wiley, 1968.

Flavell, J. H., Speer, J. R., Green, F. L., and August, D. L. "The Development of Comprehension Monitoring and Knowledge About Communication." *Monograph of the Society for Research in Child Development*, 1981, *46*, 1–65.

Flavell, J. H., and Wellman, H. M. "Metamemory." In R. V. Kail, Jr., and J. W. Hagen (Eds.), *Perspectives on the Development of Memory and Cognition*. Hillsdale, N.J.: Erlbaum, 1977.

Glucksberg, S., Krauss, R. M., and Higgins, E. T. "The Development of Referential Communication Skills." In F. D. Horowitz (Ed.), *Review of Child Development Research*, Vol. 4. Chicago: University of Chicago Press, 1975.

Glucksberg, S., Krauss, R. M., and Weisberg, R. "Referential Communication in Nursery School Children: Method and Some Preliminary Findings." *Journal of Experimental Child Psychology,* 1966, *3,* 333-342.

Gottman, J., Gonso, J., and Rasmussen, B. "Social Interaction, Social Competence, and Friendship in Children." *Child Development,* 1975, *46,* 709-718.

Higgins, E. T., Fondacaro, R., and McCann, C. D. "Rules and Roles: The 'Communication Game' and Speaker-Listener Processes." In W. P. Dickson (Ed.), *Children's Oral Communication Skills.* New York: Academic Press, 1981.

Ironsmith, M., and Whitehurst, G. J. "The Development of Listener Abilities in Communication: How Children Deal with Ambiguous Information." *Child Development,* 1978, *49,* 348-352.

Karabenick, J. D., and Miller, S. A. "The Effects of Age, Sex, and Listener Feedback on Gradeschool Children's Referential Communication." *Child Development,* 1977, *48,* 678-683.

Markman, E. M. "Comprehension Monitoring." In W. P. Dickson (Ed.), *Children's Oral Communication Skills.* New York: Academic Press, 1981.

Marvin, R. S., Greenberg, M. T., and Mossler, D. G. "The Early Development of Conceptual Perspective-Taking: Distinguishing Among Multiple Perspectives." *Child Development,* 1976, *47,* 511-514.

Miller, G. A., Galanter, E., and Pribram, K. H. *Plans and the Structure of Behavior.* New York: Holt, Rinehart and Winston, 1960.

Patterson, C. J., Cosgrove, J. M., and O'Brien, R. G. "Nonverbal Indicants of Comprehension and Noncomprehension in Children." *Developmental Psychology,* 1980, *16,* 38-48.

Patterson, C. J., and Kister, M. C. "The Development of Listener Skills for Referential Communication." In W. P. Dickson (Ed.), *Children's Oral Communication Skills.* New York: Academic Press, 1981.

Patterson, C. J., Massad, C. M., and Cosgrove, J. M. "Children's Referential Communication: Components of Plans for Effective Listening." *Developmental Psychology,* 1978, *14,* 401-406.

Patterson, C. J., O'Brien, C., Kister, M. C., Carter, D. B., and Kotsonis, M. E. "Development of Comprehension Monitoring as a Function of Context." *Developmental Psychology,* 1981, *17,* 379-389.

Peterson, C. L., Danner, F. W., and Flavell, J. H. "Developmental Changes in Children's Responses to Three Indications of Communicative Failure." *Child Development,* 1972, *43,* 1463-1468.

Pratt, M. W., and Bates, K. R. "Young Editors: Preschoolers' Evaluation and Production of Ambiguous Messages." *Developmental Psychology,* 1982, *18,* 30-42.

Pratt, M. W., Scribner, S., and Cole, M. "Children as Teachers: Developmental Studies of Instructional Communication." *Child Development,* 1977, *48,* 1475-1481.

Roberts, R. J., Jr. "Errors and the Assessment of Cognitive Development." In K. W. Fischer (Ed.), *New Directions for Child Development: Cognitive Development,* no. 12. San Francisco: Jossey-Bass, 1981.

Roberts, R. J., Jr., and Patterson, C. J. "Perspective-Taking and Referential Communication: The Question of Correspondence Reconsidered." *Child Development,* in press.

Robinson, E. J., and Robinson, W. P. "Children's Explanations of Communication Failure and the Inadequacy of the Misunderstood Message." *Developmental Psychology,* 1977a, *13,* 156-161.

Robinson, E. J., and Robinson, W. P. "Development in the Understanding of Causes of Success and Failure in Verbal Communication." *Cognition,* 1977b, *5,* 363–378.

Robinson, E. J., and Robinson, W. P. "Development of Understanding About Communication: Message Inadequacy and Its Role in Causing Communication Failure." *Genetic Psychology Monographs,* 1978, *98,* 233–279.

Robinson, E. J. "The Child's Understanding of Inadequate Messages and Communication Failure: A Problem of Ignorance or Egocentrism?" In W. P. Dickson (Ed.), *Children's Oral Communication Skills.* New York: Academic Press, 1981.

Schmidt, C., and Paris, S. "The Development of Children's Oral Communication Skills." In L. P. Reese and C. C. Lipsitt (Eds.), *Advances in Child Development and Behavior.* New York: Academic Press, 1982.

Shantz, C. U. "The Role of Role-Taking in Children's Referential Communication." In W. P. Dickson (Ed.), *Children's Oral Communication Skills.* New York: Academic Press, 1981.

Shatz, M. "The Relationship Between Cognitive Processes and the Development of Communication Skills." In B. Keasey (Ed.), *Nebraska Symposium on Motivation, 1977.* Lincoln: University of Nebraska Press, 1978.

Singer, J. B., and Flavell, J. H. "Development of Knowledge About Communication: Children's Evaluations of Explicitly Ambiguous Messages." *Child Development,* 1981, *52,* 1211–1215.

Urbain, E. S., and Kendall, P. C. "Review of Social-Cognitive Problem-Solving Interventions with Children." *Psychological Bulletin,* 1980, *88,* 109–143.

Vurpillot, E. "The Development of Scanning Strategies and Their Relation to Visual Differentiation." *Journal of Experimental Child Psychology,* 1968, *6,* 632–650.

Whitehurst, G. J. "The Development of Communication: Changes with Age and Modeling." *Child Development,* 1976, *47,* 473–482.

Whitehurst, G. J., and Sonnenschein, S. "The Development of Communication: Attribute Variation Leads to Contrast Failure." *Journal of Experimental Child Psychology,* 1978, *25,* 454–490.

Whitehurst, G. J., and Sonnenschein, S. "The Development of Informative Messages in Referential Communication: Knowing When Versus Knowing How." In W. P. Dickson (Ed.), *Children's Oral Communication Skills.* New York: Academic Press, 1981.

Charlotte J. Patterson is associate professor of psychology at the University of Virginia.

Ralph J. Roberts, Jr., is a doctoral candidate in psychology at the University of Virginia.

*The ability to agree on plans for reunion seems to be instrumental
in facilitating comfortable separations between mothers and
late-preschool-aged children. This development in patterns of separation behavior
is interpreted in terms of symbolic-thought development and the
increased sense of importance of abstract plans for behavior.*

Preschoolers' Changing Conceptions of Their Mothers: A Social-Cognitive Study of Mother–Child Attachment

Robert S. Marvin
Mark T. Greenberg

Recently there has been increasing interest in the question of parent–child attachment beyond infancy and early childhood (Blehar, 1974; Blurton Jones and Leach, 1972; Lieberman, 1977; Moscowitz, Schwartz, and Corsini, 1977). With few exceptions, however (for example, Feldman and Ingham, 1975; Maccoby and Feldman, 1972; Marvin, 1977), these studies have been primarily focused on comparing treatment groups, such as daycare versus home-reared, or on behavior with mother versus behavior with peers, rather

This research was supported by grants from the William T. Grant Foundation and the Spencer Foundation. This chapter was presented in abbreviated form, and with reversed authorship, at the Southeastern Conference on Human Development, Atlanta, April 1978. We would like to thank Charlotte J. Patterson and Eleanor Maccoby for their helpful comments and suggestions. Reprint requests should be sent to Robert S. Marvin, Department of Psychology, Gilmer Hall, University of Virginia, Charlottesville, VA 22901.

than describing postinfancy normative developmental changes in attachment interactions. This focus can be attributed primarily to the lack of a conceptual framework within which to examine and explain these changes. The measurement of attachment through motor behaviors, which is customary in research with infants, may not be sufficient with these older children (for example, see Cohen, 1974). To fully understand attachment interactions between older preschoolers and their parents, it is also necessary to examine children's cognitive and communicative activities and the roles these activities play in structuring such interactions.

The models we construct to understand children's interactions and relationships should acknowledge that, as children develop, their relationships become regulated by increasingly abstract factors. Among these factors is the older child's tendency to respond not only to another person's behavior but also to his or her conception of the other's attitudes, intentions, or plans. This tendency allows a degree of negotiation and cooperation not available to younger children and serves as the cognitive-communicative basis for much more sophisticated and smoothly operating relationships.

It is likely that the first relationships within which children develop this skill are with their attachment figures and that these skills develop near the end of the preschool years. We believe it is particularly important to adopt such a social-cognitive approach to studying parent–child attachment in this age range; doing so may resolve the paradox that, while a child and a parent are separating and "individuating" (Mahler, Pine, and Bergman, 1975), at the same time their relationship is becoming more intimate in other ways. In this chapter, we draw on Bowlby's (1969) theory to examine the attachment between parent and preschool child from a social-cognitive perspective. (We also believe this model has important implications for other developing relationships, such as those with peers.)

Bowlby proposed that, between late infancy and the end of the preschool years, two qualitative changes take place in the attachment between mother and child, and each change leads to more complex and subtle forms of mother–child behavioral integration. Some time between six and eight months of age (the beginning of Phase III), children develop a "set goal," or cognitive representation, of a variable but specified degree of physical proximity or contact with the mother, as well as a set of behavioral plans for purposefully achieving the corresponding goal-state. These children are able to take much more initiative in controlling proximity with their mothers than was possible earlier.

As the child's communicative competence increases, mother and child become able to communicate their goals and plans to one another verbally and nonverbally. This leads to decreased distress in two- and three-year-olds during brief separations (Maccoby and Feldman, 1972; Marvin, 1977; Weinraub and Lewis, 1977); presumably, the child now understands and trusts that the mother will return. Until some time after the third birthday, however, the child usually continues to seek the mother's proximity upon reunion (Marvin, 1977).

Bowlby suggests that these younger preschoolers still have major difficulties in engaging in the reciprocal process of communicating goals and plans. The problem concerns the "working model," or conception, of the mother. Specifically, young preschoolers are inept at estimating others' points of view—for example, their plans, goals, and feelings—and at thinking about causal factors in the behavior of others (see Livesley and Bromley, 1973; Shantz, 1975). These limitations make it difficult for the mother-child dyad to exploit one of the major advantages of human communication—the construction and execution of joint goals and plans.

As children come to see that others' perspectives are independent of and potentially different from their own, and as they become able to make simple (but increasingly complex) inferences about the behavior of others, a significant change takes place in the mother-child relationship. At least in relatively simple (and psychologically important) situations, children can now recognize when their mothers' goals or plans are the same as or different from their own. The possibility now arises of mother and child actively and intentionally constructing a joint or mutually agreed-upon plan of interaction. This can be accomplished by one of them suggesting a plan agreed upon by the other or through a process of mutual negotiation followed by agreement. Bowlby proposes that the mother-child relationship changes at this point to Phase IV, the "goal-corrected partnership." He sees Phases III and IV as two distinct cognitive-behavioral organizations in the development of mother-child attachment beyond infancy—the young child, who is merely able to maintain proximity in an intentional fashion, versus the older preschooler, who is also able to construct and maintain intentionally joint plans for regulating proximity. Ainsworth and others (1978) identified three major individual differences between the ways one- and two-year-olds regulate proximity to their mothers upon reunion: secure proximity-seeking (Type A); avoidant (Type B); and ambivalent (Type C).

In an extension of Bowlby's model, Marvin (1977) proposes that, with the onset of Phase IV, child and mother should come to attach less importance than before to physical proximity with one another. The maintenance of joint goals and plans now becomes one of the child's set-goals (presumably this has been one of mother's goals all along—see Maccoby, 1978). It now becomes possible for children to realize that they share with their mothers a relationship that is not totally dependent on interaction within physical proximity. That is, mother and child can now share a joint goal or plan whether they are together or apart, and the child thus realizes that the relationship continues even when they are separated. This realization should allow children to feel much more secure during brief separations, as long as they perceive their mothers and themselves as sharing joint goals and plans and so long as children usually shared in their construction. Rather than becoming upset by brief separations per se, these older preschoolers will become upset when they perceive a lack of joint goals or plans in regulating separations and reunions.

Marvin (1977) observed a sample of two-, three-, and four-year-olds in a laboratory interaction that involved brief separations between mother and child. The results indicated that most four-year-olds attempted to construct joint or mutually agreed-upon plans with their mothers regarding separation and subsequent reunion. The four-year-olds' responses to separation and reunion varied according to whether a joint plan was reached. If such a plan had been constructed, the child tended to remain happy and secure during the separation, responded to the mother's return in a sociable and relaxed manner, and did not seek her proximity. If a joint plan had not been reached — that is, if the child had not eventually agreed to the mother's departure — the child tended to be upset during the separation and to respond to the mother's return by behaving in an angry, controlling manner. Most of the four-year-olds also performed in a non-egocentric fashion on a number of perspective-taking tasks. Finally, the results indicated that the two- or three-year-old child tended to respond egocentrically to the perspective-taking tasks and to display the same Phase III reunion patterns as those identified by Ainsworth and others (1978). The results for the four-year-olds were experimentally replicated in a subsequent study (Marvin and VanDevender, 1978). Moreover, Greenberg and Marvin (1979) found in a sample of the profoundly deaf child that attainment of the goal-corrected partnership was related to the mother–child dyad's level of communicative competence, rather than merely to age.

While these studies suggest a relationship between developmental changes in attachment behavior and certain social-cognitive skills, there has been no direct test of this relationship, nor of the related change in children's conceptions of factors controlling their mothers' behavior. The purpose of the present study was to investigate the relationship between attainment of the Phase IV goal-corrected partnership and children's conceptions of factors controlling their mothers' behavior during attachment interactions. Children must objectively understand the independence of participants' points of view to participate actively in negotiating common goals and plans with others. Furthermore, they must understand that others' behavior is controlled by others' plans, rather than by the children's own. This should lead the participants to seek information from one another indicating that their goals or plans do mesh.

Accordingly, our expectation was that children who had accurate conceptions of factors controlling their mothers' behavior would respond to brief separations according to the logic of the Phase IV goal-corrected partnership. Those children who had inaccurate conceptions of these factors were expected to respond according to the logic of Phase III. The attachment interactions were recorded during a laboratory interaction that involved brief separations, and the children's conceptions of their mothers were investigated through direct questioning during one of these separations.

We see this design as an important addition to methodological alternatives for research on social-cognitive development. To be more specific, most studies that attempt to relate social-cognitive measures to measures of social interaction employ each measure in different physical and temporal contexts—for example, perspective-taking measures in experimental tasks and social-interaction measures in home or playground settings on different days. In this study, we obtained both measures in the same context during the very time when the children would theoretically have been expected to behave spontaneously on the basis of both skills. While this design raises certain problems (especially, perhaps, with preschoolers), we are convinced that the increased validity that results from obtaining both measures in the same context is more than adequate compensation.

Method

Subjects

Thirty-two three- and four-year-old children were observed, sixteen of each age. In all cases, the children were observed within one month of their birthdays. Each age group contained equal numbers of boys and girls. The children were from middle-class families living in a residential section of a large city. (This sample is a subsample of that reported in Marvin, 1977.)

Procedures

Strange Situation. Each mother–child pair was observed in a "strange situation," a standardized twenty-one-minute, eight-episode situation involving two brief separations between mother and child (Ainsworth and Wittig, 1969; Ainsworth and others, 1978). The room contained chairs for the mother, the child, and a stranger; pieces of furniture; toys; and a one-way window, through which the entire event was videotaped. Since phase-of-attachment categorizations required the child to be left alone, only the final three episodes are considered relevant to this study. The possibility that any analysis might be confounded by earlier episodes is remote, since all the children went through the same eight episodes. (The earlier four episodes can be summarized as follows: mother and child present; mother, child, and stranger present; child and stranger present; and mother and child present.)

Episode 6: Child Alone. The mother says, per instructions, "I have to make a phone call. I'll be back." If the child objects as the mother leaves, she tells her child that he or she must remain in the room and that she will be back. Many of the mothers said more—suggesting play activities, expanding on the purpose of departure, trying to get children to agree to the departure, and so forth. The mother leaves and closes the door; the child is alone for three minutes. If the child bcomes very distressed, the episode is terminated.

Episode 7: Child and Stranger Present. A friendly female adult stranger, with whom the child has spent six minutes earlier in the situation (Episodes 3 and 4; see Ainsworth and others, 1978), enters the room, plays with the child for approximately one minute, and then asks the child a series of questions about his or her conception of the mother's departure and return. This episode also lasts for three minutes.

Separation questions. During the last two minutes of Episode 7, the stranger asks the child if he or she would like to answer some questions. The questions are asked in a gentle manner (the stranger has been instructed to cease questioning and reassure the child if he or she becomes upset). As it turned out, this was unnecessary; no children were upset by the questions.

The questions, and the order in which they were asked, are as follows:

Question A: "Where's Mommy?"
Question B: "Will Mommy come back?"

Questions A and B were asked to familiarize the child with the questioning procedure, to establish his or her linguistic ability to answer such questions, and to ensure that he or she remembered where the mother was and that she would return. (Since no logical inferences were required for answering these questions, they will not be included in the analyses.) Except for three who did not answer any questions, all the children answered these two questions correctly. The following questions were used in the analysis:

Question 1: "How do you know Mommy will come back?"
    This question was asked to see if the child would refer back to the process gone through with the mother in discussing and planning her departure and return.
Question 2: "Can *you* make Mommy come back?"
    This question assessed the child's ability to recognize that (1) it was the mother herself, rather than the child, who was in direct control of the mother's behavior, and/or (2) the child could indirectly control the mother's behavior through some specified behavior of his or her own.
Question 3: "What if Mommy didn't want to come back? Would Mommy come back even if she didn't want to?"
    Here, the child was required to accept a hypothetical perspective on the mother's part—a perspective presumably in direct opposition to what the child would want it to be—and to make a logical inference about the mother's behavior on the basis of that hypothetical perspective.

After the child finished responding to Question 3, the stranger spoke with him or her for a few moments about how both of them knew that the mother did, in fact, want to come back.

Episode 8: Mother and Child Present. The mother reenters the room and greets her child. The stranger leaves and the mother sits in her chair, responding in any manner she wishes to her child's initiatives. After three minutes, the situation is terminated.

Methods of Analysis

Strange Situation. On the basis of an inventory of more than fifty discrete behaviors, the videotapes were transcribed, with each behavior coded in the order in which it occurred. Verbal interactions during the mother's departure, the separation, and the reunion were coded verbatim. Further data reduction consisted of grouping these behaviors into discrete classes, coding the classes in their temporal order, and then categorizing each child as being in either Phase III or Phase IV of attachment development. The classes of behavior relevant to this report are as follows.

Preseparation Behavior

Agree to the Mother's Departure. The child and the mother actively construct a joint plan for separation and reunion, and/or the child gives any verbal or nonverbal indication of agreement concerning the separation—for example, "Okay," "Yes" (if the mother asks if it's okay); nods head.

Protest the Mother's Departure. This includes any verbal or nonverbal indication that the child does not want the mother to leave or that the child wants to accompany her. Some children initially protested, but subsequently agreed after extended discussion. For this reason, the final scoring of agreement/protest was based on the child's last relevant communication prior to the mother's departure.

No Response to the Mother's Departure. The child may watch the mother while she explains her departure and leaves, but makes no response, thus neither agreeing nor protesting.

Behavior While Alone

Distress, with Little or no Play. The child is distressed (cries, fusses, and/or displays a "cry-face") for more than five seconds during the separation and engages in no more than intermittent exploratory play.

Play, with no Distress. The child engages in exploratory play while alone (Episode 6), exhibiting no distress when the mother first departs and no distress for more than five seconds during the entire episode.

Reunion Behavior

Approach the Mother. The child locomotes to within arm's reach of the mother within fifteen seconds of her return. Since this classification was intended to include approaches for the sake of proximity, rather than for the sake of playful interaction, approaches were not scored when they were accompanied or immediately followed by sociable behavior toward the mother.

Avoid the Mother. Within fifteen seconds of the mother's return, the child either does not acknowledge her return or does so only with a short glance followed by gaze aversion. The child may also ignore the mother's requests for interaction or proximity and/or increase distance from her.

Sociable Behavior. Within fifteen seconds of the mother's return, the child carries on a pleasant conversation with her or interacts with her happily in the context of some game or use of the toys.

Controlling Behavior. In a whining tone of voice, the child either verbally refuses to engage in some interaction or play suggested by the mother and verbally insists on some other activity or makes repeated verbal demands of the mother and is not satisfied when or if the mother is unable to fulfill them immediately.

Once all the behaviors were classified in their appropriate temporal order, the children were categorized according to phase of attachment. Children were categorized as having a Phase IV goal-corrected partnership with their mothers if they either (1) constructed and/or agreed upon a plan with the mother regarding her departure and return, played while alone without distress, and responded to her return in a sociable manner without approach or controlling behavior; or (2) actively protested the mother's plan for the separation (that is, failed to construct a joint plan), displayed distress while alone, and responded to reunion by behaving toward the mother in a whining, verbally controlling manner (with or without approach).

Children were categorized as being in Phase III if they (1) approached the mother when she returned, but did not display any controlling behavior, whether or not they had previously agreed with her departure; (2) avoided the mother when she returned; or (3) protested the mother's departure but, displayed sociable behavior toward her when she returned, with no controlling behavior. This last pattern was assigned to the Phase III category because it does not clearly possess the organization of either the third or fourth phase of the model (one three-year-old displayed this pattern). We chose to be conservative in assigning children to the fourth phase.

Separation Questions. The children's responses to each question were descriptively classified as either correct or incorrect, depending on whether their answers were based on the planning activity the dyad had engaged in prior to the mother' departure and/or reflected awareness that the mother's behavior was directly controlled by her perspective, rather than the children's own. The range and classification of answers actually obtained are as follows:

Question 1: "How do you know Mommy will come back?"
    Correct: "Because she told me"; "Because she said she would"; "Because she said she was gonna come back."
    Incorrect: "I don't know"; "I just know"; "Because"; "I just do"; "I got to know"; "The door isn't open yet"; "Because of the airplane."
Question 2: "Can *you* make Mommy come back?"
    Correct: "No"; "No, can you?"; "No, but herself can"; "Yes" (specifies a reasonable behavior when asked *how* he or she can make Mommy come back—for example, "I'd yell for her"; "I'd go get her").
    Incorrect: "Yes"; nods.

Question 3: "What if Mommy didn't want to come back? Would Mommy come back even if she didn't want to?"
Correct: "No"; "Mommy will come back if she wants to."
Incorrect: "Yes"; nods; "Mommy will come back"; "Mommy wants to."

The classification for Question 3 might at first appear subject to the criticism that the probable response by older children and adults would be "Yes, Mommy would come back anyway," but we propose that the latter response would be derived from a reasoning process more complex than the evidence suggests is available to four-year-old children—that is, reasoning about the relative priority of two or more goals and/or engaging in recursive thinking (for example, Miller, Kessel, and Flavell, 1970). To a four-year-old, the world is not so complex. The evidence suggests that these children should operate on the simple premise that the mother does not want to come back, realize that her behavior is controlled by her own desires, and conclude that she would not come back. As will be seen in the section on results, this proposal is supported by the patterns of children's responses to all three separation questions.

The children were assigned a summary score of *correct* if they answered two or three of the questions correctly and a summary score of *incorrect* if they answered fewer than two correctly. These summary scores were then compared with the classifications obtained from the "strange situation."

Results

Coder Agreement. Coder-agreement measures were computed at two levels of coding—sequential classes of behavior and categorization of the children into either Phase III or Phase IV of Bowlby's model. Two coders independently completed all classifications and categorizations. Coder agreement was computed on the basis of the number of agreements divided by the number of agreements + disagreements. For the nine classes of behavior, coder agreement was .95; for the attachment categorizations, .97.

Behavior During the First Separation. Since the results are based on the second separation and reunion, it is necessary to provide a summary of the children's behavior during the first separation (Episodes 3 and 4). By the end of Episode 3, 81 percent of the three-year-olds and 87 percent of the four-year-olds were interacting sociably with the stranger (Greenberg and Marvin, in press). During the first separation, the stranger was present, and none of the children showed overt distress concerning the mother's absence (one child of each age ignored the stranger during this episode). There were no age differences in reactions to the stranger, and 91 percent of the children displayed consistent reactions across Episodes 3, 4, and 7. Thus, age differences both in response to the second separation and the separation questions are not an artifact of behavior earlier in the situation.

Phase of Attachment. Twelve of the sixteen three-year-olds were categorized as being in Phase III of attachment development, and four three-year-olds were categorized as being in the Phase IV goal-corrected partnership. Of the sixteen four-year-olds, four were categorized as being in Phase III and twelve as being in Phase IV. This age difference is significant ($x^2 = 8.00$, $dF = 1$, $p < .01$).

Responses to Separation Questions. As anticipated, a few children (one three-year-old and two four-year-olds) completely rejected the stranger in the mother's absence and refused to answer the questions, but none of the children who did answer the questions appeared upset by them. Although six children answered too few questions to receive a summary score, there appears to be no particular bias to their distribution across age, question, or phase of attachment.

As Table 1 indicates, the three-year-olds tended to answer Questions 1, 2, and 3 incorrectly, while the four-year-olds tended to answer correctly. The age differences were significant for all three questions, as well as for the summary scores: Question 1 ($p = .002$, Fisher's Exact Test); Question 2 ($x^2 = 6.04$, $dF = 1$, $p < .025$); and Question 3 ($p = .002$, Fisher's Exact Test).

Our view that "no" is the correct answer to Question 3 (the rationale of which is presented in the section on methods) is also supported by the age difference in responses to Question 3 and by individual response patterns to all three questions. Of the eight children who answered Question 3 in the negative, none received a score of *incorrect* on either of the other two questions. Of the sixteen children answering this question in the affirmative, fourteen received scores of *incorrect* on at least one of the other two questions ($p < .001$,

Table 1. Relationship Between Age and Response to Separation Questions

	Age 3	Age 4
Question 1		
Correct	0	9
Incorrect	11	4
No Answer	5	3
Question 2		
Correct	2	10
Incorrect	9	3
No Answer	5	3
Question 3		
Correct	0	8
Incorrect	11	5
No or unscorable answer	5	3
Summary Score		
Correct	0	10
Incorrect	12	4
Unscorable	4	2

Fisher's Exact Test). Finally, those children who responded to Question 3 in the affirmative tended to do so immediately, while those responding in the negative hesitated for a few moments before answering. It appeared that the latter children were engaging in some extended logical process, whereas the former were not (see Greenberg, Marvin, and Mossler, 1977).

Relationship Between Separation Questions and Phase of Attachment. Using the summary scores for the separation questions, a within-subjects comparison was made of the relationship between phase of attachment and the questions. As Table 2 indicates, there is a strong relationship between the two measures. Almost all the Phase III children performed incorrectly on the questions, whereas most of the Phase IV children performed correctly ($p = .007$, Fisher's Exact Test). This relationship remains significant even when unscorable children are treated as incorrect ($x^2 = 7.12$, $dF = 1$, $p < .01$). Had the more stringent criterion of three correct answers been used for a summary score of *correct*, two more children categorized as being in Phase IV would have received scores of *incorrect*. This comparison would still have been significant ($p = .03$, Fisher's Exact Test).

Discussion

The results of this study extend recent evidence that children as young as four years of age are able to make objective conceptual judgments about aspects of others that are not available to direct perception—for example, others' thoughts, motivational states, and knowledge states (see Marvin, Greenberg, and Mossler, 1976; Urberg and Docherty, 1976). The results of the separation questions indicate that at this age children are beginning to develop objective conceptions of the causal relationship between the mother's perspective and her behavior and to realize that they can reason about this relationship in a logical, reversible manner, even when the conclusion is contrary to their own desires.

The relation between phase of attachment and summary scores for the separation questions suggests that the developing ability to reason objectively about causal bases of the mother's behavior is related both to developmental changes in the child's reaction to brief separations and, more generally, to

Table 2. Relationship Between Phase of Attachment and Summary Score

Summary Score	Phase III	Phase IV
Correct	1	9
Incorrect	11	5
Unscorable	4	2

changes in the ways mother and child regulate proximity between them. Children who answered the separation questions correctly attempted to construct a joint plan with their mothers concerning her departure. If the attempt was successful, the children were relaxed and sociable upon reunion. If the attempt was unsuccessful, the children were distressed and controlling upon reunion and presumably behaved in this way in an attempt to re-establish their own control within the interaction (Marvin, 1977).

The children who answered the questions incorrectly did not organize their behavior on the basis of jointly constructed plans. They tended either to protest, give no response, or talk about the separation without reaching either agreement or disagreement. When the mother returned, these children behaved sociably toward her and/or sought or avoided her proximity. Thus, these children behaved in a manner similar to one- and two-year-olds in the same situation.

As Table 2 indicates, there were some exceptions to these stated results. Most of these occurred among the three-year-old children who were categorized as being in Phase IV but received summary scores of *incorrect* on the separation questions. One hypothesis for these exceptions is that both measures are related to age, rather than to each other. This possibility is suggested by the fact that no three-year-old, regardless of attachment phase, received a summary score of *correct* on the separation questions. Nevertheless, the relationship is not merely an age-related phenomenon; in addition to the logical problems involved in such a hypothesis, the results indicated that four of the four-year-olds answered the questions incorrectly, and all these children were in Phase III. Thus, while answering the questions correctly may be age-related to a certain extent, it is certainly related to the development of the goal-corrected partnership. A second and related hypothesis is that there is a transitional development period during which children can behave according to the logic of a goal-corrected partnership, but do not yet have the cognitive and linguistic skills necessary to use such logic in a way that would enable them to answer the questions correctly (compare Piaget, 1976).

One question this study did not address concerns the role played by differential quality of the mother–child attachment. Older preschoolers who are less secure in their attachment will probably be less likely to agree to a separation and more likely to display verbally controlling behavior upon reunion. In fact, the two Phase IV patterns, both of which reflect the social-cognitive change proposed earlier, may serve as one basis for identifying individual differences in quality of mother–child attachment in older preschoolers. This study, however, focused on developmental differences; further research will be required to examine individual variations within this general developmental theme.

This study has focused specifically on attachment interactions, but both objective reasoning about the behavior of others and the attendant process of joint planning should be viewed as general-purpose skills leading to greater synchrony in all types of interactions. Children's ability to evaluate the degree of match between their own goals and plans and those of others allows children to attempt alignment of the two perspectives—all before beginning the relevant interaction (compare Miller, Galanter, and Pribram, 1960; Piaget and Inhelder, 1969). If this attempt is unsuccessful and if the alignment is emotionally salient to the child then distress and mother–child conflict are the likely results. This is certainly a form of cooperation characteristic of most close adult interpersonal relationships.

Finally, the results of this study indicate the value of a social-cognitive approach to studying developing interpersonal interactions and relationships. They also indicate that temporal sequences of social interaction, as well as hypothesized cognitive processes and mechanisms, can be described and categorized within the same general theoretical and methodological framework. Only through such attempts to integrate traditionally disparate areas of developmental psychology will we come to understand how diverse elements combine to create a unitary, functioning child within the network of interpersonal relationships.

References

Ainsworth, M. D. S., and Wittig, B. A. "Attachment and Exploratory Behavior of One-Year-Olds in a Strange Situation." In B. M. Foss (Ed.), *Determinants of Infant Behavior.* Vol. IV. New York: Wiley, 1969.

Ainsworth, M. D. S., Blehar, M. C., Waters, E., and Wall, S. *Patterns of Attachment: A Psychological Study of the Strange Situation.* Hillsdale, N.J.: Erlbaum, 1978.

Blehar, M. C. "Anxious Attachment and Defensive Reactions Associated with Day Care." *Child Development,* 1974, *45,* 683-692.

Blurton Jones, N., and Leach, G. "Behavior of Children and Their Mothers at Separation and Greeting." In N. Blurton Jones (Ed.), *Ethological Studies of Child Behavior.* London: Cambridge University Press, 1972.

Bowlby, J. *Attachment and Loss.* Vol. 1: *Attachment.* New York: Basic Books, 1969.

Cohen, L. J. "The Operational Definition of Human Attachment." *Psychological Bulletin,* 1974, *81,* 207-217.

Feldman, S. S., and Ingham, M. E. "Attachment Behavior: A Validation Study in Two Age Groups." *Child Development,* 1975, *46,* 319-330.

Greenberg, M. T., and Marvin, R. S. "Attachment Patterns in Profoundly Deaf Preschool Children." *Merrill-Palmer Quarterly,* 1979, *25* (4), 265-279.

Greenberg, M. T., and Marvin, R. S. "Reactions of Preschool Children to an Adult Stranger: A Behavioral Systems Approach." *Child Development,* in press.

Greenberg, M. T., Marvin, R. S., and Mossler, D. G. "The Development of Conditional Reasoning Skills." *Developmental Psychology,* 1977, *13,* 527-528.

Lieberman, A. F. "Preschoolers' Competence with a Peer: Relations with Attachment and Peer Experience." *Child Development,* 1977, *48* (4), 1277-1287.

Livesley, W. G., and Bromley, D. B. *Person Perception in Childhood and Adolescence.* London: Wiley, 1973.

Maccoby, E. E. "Developmental Change in the Nature and Function of Parent–Child Interaction." Paper presented as part of a symposium on "The Family: Setting Priorities," Washington, D. C., May 1978.

Maccoby, E. E., and Feldman, S. S. "Mother-Attachment and Stranger-Reactions in the Third Year of Life." *Monographs of the Society for Research in Child Development,* 1972, *37,* Serial no. 146.

Mahler, M. S., Pine, F., and Bergman, A. *The Psychological Birth of the Human Infant.* New York: Basic Books, 1975.

Marvin, R. S. "An Ethological-Cognitive Model for the Attenuation of Mother–Child Attachment Behavior." In T. M. Alloway and L. Krames (Eds.), *Advances in the Study of Communication and Affect.* Vol. 3. *The Development of Social Attachments.* New York: Plenum Press, 1977.

Marvin, R. S., Greenberg, M. T., and Mossler, D. G. "The Early Development of Conceptual Perspective-Taking: Distinguishing Among Multiple Perspectives." *Child Development,* 1976, *47,* 511–514.

Marvin, R. S., and VanDevender, T. L. *An Experimental Study of Brief Separations Between Mothers and Their Four-Year-Old Children.* Unpublished manuscript, University of Virginia, 1978.

Miller, G. A., Gallanter, E., and Pribram, K. H. *Plans and the Structure of Behavior.* New York: Holt, Rinehart and Winston, 1960.

Miller, P. H., Kessel, F. S., and Flavell, J. H. "Thinking About People Thinking About People Thinking About. . . : A Study in Social Cognitive Development." *Child Development,* 1970, *41,* 613–623.

Moscowitz, D. S., Schwartz, J. C., and Corsini, D. A. "Initiating Day Care at Three Years of Age: Effects on Attachment." *Child Development,* 1977, *48,* 1271–1276.

Piaget, J. *The Grasp of Consciousness: Action and Concept in the Young Child.* Cambridge: Harvard University Press, 1976.

Piaget, J., and Inhelder, B. *The Psychology of the Child.* New York: Basic Books, 1969.

Shantz, C. U. "The Development of Social Cognition." In E. M. Hetherington (Ed.), *Review of Child Development Research.* Vol. 5. Chicago: University of Chicago Press, 1975.

Urberg, K. A., and Docherty, E. M. "Development of Role-Taking Skills in Young Children." *Developmental Psychology,* 1976, *12,* 198–203.

Weinraub, M., and Lewis, M. "The Determinants of Children's Responses to Separation." *Monographs of the Society for Research in Child Development,* 1977, *12* (42), Serial no. 172.

Robert S. Marvin is director of the Department of Pediatric Psychology for the Children's Rehabilitation Center at the University of Virginia Medical Center.

Mark T. Greenberg is an assistant professor of psychology at the University of Washington.

An analysis of children's strategies for joining playmates' activities reveals age- and sex-linked differences in affiliative planning. Differential rates of development in the structure of entry strategies are reported.

Children's Plans for Joining Play: An Analysis of Structure and Function

David L. Forbes
Mary Maxwell Katz
Barry Paul
David Lubin

Researchers studying children's social-reasoning ability have made great strides toward understanding how children perceive and think about their social worlds. Starting from a point just over a decade ago, when researchers had only global ideas about the nature of social–cognitive skills, we have proceeded to the point where a diverse array of qualitatively distinct social-reasoning components have been identified and studied.

A relatively recent addition to the list of skills under study is the capacity for planning in social situations. Students investigating children's social

This research was supported by grants from the National Science Foundation (BNS-78-19119) and the National Institute of Mental Health (1-R01-MH34723). Requests for reprints should be addressed to David Forbes at the Peer Interaction Project, 510 Larsen Hall, Harvard Graduate School of Education, Appian Way, Cambridge, MA 02138.

D. Forbes and M. T. Greenberg, *New Directions for Child Development:*
Children's Planning Strategies, no. 18. San Francisco: Jossey-Bass, December 1982. **61**

planning have concerned themselves with the ways children think about social action and interaction and have then distinguished their work from past efforts, which examined thinking about moral principles, social institutions, social relationships, and general qualities of persons. This change in emphasis may be attributed to an interest in directly studying reasoning as it may function in regulating behavior, and, thus, to an interest in dynamic reasoning processes, rather than relatively static ones.

Students of children's social planning have benefited from some past work on general aspects of children's planning, projects that focused on the planning process per se, independent of interest in particular content areas for plans (such as social interaction, for example). Most of this work (Klahr and Robinson, 1981; Siegler, 1981) has investigated children's behavior in laboratory problem-solving situations, to learn more about the development of the cognitive processes required for any task of plan formulation and execution. An important aspect of this work has been learning about the development of metaplanning, the process by which individuals reflect upon and organize their thoughts and actions to make and carry out plans in a particular situation (compare Pea, this volume). Results have highlighted gaps in the metaplanning of children (and of adults, too, in some cases), gaps related to weighing priorities and assessing alternative procedures before acting.

Researchers (for example, Nelson and Gruendel, 1979) have also examined knowledge about behavioral events in everyday life (such as baking a cake) to tell us more about the structure of how children remember plans, or "scripts," for behavior. From this work, we have learned that children may only gradually acquire the ability to store plans that are organized on multiple levels. Subordinate and superordinate steps in such plans are often reported in a confused fashion by young children, and their idiosyncratic organization of plan memory may include some important procedural steps while omitting others.

Other projects (for example, Forbes and Lubin, 1981) have examined how children think about the ways their behaviors affect people around them and have shown an interest in documenting children's understanding of how planning can solve social problems or further goals in social situations. This work has suggested that children initially have very magical beliefs about how they may influence others and only gradually grow to understand how others perceive and uniquely react to their actions. Still other researchers have explored children's knowledge of the implicit rules that may shape interactions with others. This research has attempted to chart the acquisition of consensual knowledge, which may affect planning behavior (Bates, 1976; Dodge, 1980). This work also shows that children can be surprisingly sophisticated in acquiring some very subtle rules for behavior, such as when to break up a fight, while at the same time they show marked primitivity in their understanding of less subtle rules, such as how to be polite. Finally, some researchers (Garvey, 1974, 1975; Haslett, 1980) have made in-depth examinations of individual child–child interactions, looking for evidence of planning in everyday life. Some of these investigations focus on conformity between observed patterns of dyadic interaction in children and abstract rules of plans, proposed as descriptions of interaction between mature individuals (compare Dore, 1977; Lakoff, 1973, for examples of such abstract rules). Remarkable orderliness in the conversations of even preschool-aged children has been suggested by this line of inquiry, indicating that children's social behavior may be governed by rule-like propensities for action, even before children can report knowledge of such rules. Other studies have developed a statistical–descriptive approach to the analysis of social-behavior sequences (for example, Bakeman and Brownlee, 1980; Gottman, 1979; Putallaz and Gottman, 1981), in the interest of documenting predictable empirical regularities in the ordering of behavior, which could support an inference of underlying concern for planning. This work has supported the results of more inferential and descriptive endeavors by establishing regularities in the organization of children's actions across large aggregated samples, again suggesting the presence of planlike orderliness, if not active planning per se.

In this chapter, we shall present a study of planning in children's social interaction. This research also focuses on evidence of planning concerns in the structure of behavior and differs from past work on this topic in two ways. First, we have employed a technique of analyzing behavior that is inherently sequential in nature. Our examination of the behaviors that began interaction sequences interpreted the role of various actions in initiating interactions and recoded these behaviors as "opening moves." Our examination of behaviors that occurred later in interactions combined information about the morphology of behavior with the behavior's context, and "midgame move" codes were developed to classify these in-context behaviors. Unlike past studies, which have categorized behavior on its morphology alone and then studied sequences of such morphological behaviors, our investigation may assign very different meanings to behaviors of a given morphological type, depending on the interactive context in which they occur.

The most important result of this strategy is that we have paid explicit attention in our coded descriptions to the assumption that behaviors are strategic and bound by context. If the interest in sequential organization is left to be addressed separately from the interpretation of individual behaviors, then what we view as the fundamentally strategic quality of behavior (derived from the premise that behavior is organized) may be lost.

A second way in which our study differs from past studies is that ours places direct emphasis on investigating the goals that inform planning behavior in social contexts. Kaplan (1974) has noted that it is inappropriate to speak of "developed" versus "underdeveloped" entities from a purely structural standpoint. He argues persuasively that it is only the assessment of structure with respect to function that can illuminate patterns of development. Thus, we have attempted to make a distinction between two basic functions that may be served by children's affiliative behavior—a child's desire to join an activity of playmates versus the child's desire to enter into a social relationship with playmates.

Our choice of the goals "joining an activity" versus "entering into a social relationship" reflects, first, our desire to focus on what are intuitively the most likely alternative explanations of "joining" behavior; that is, we believe that attributing our observed-behavior data to one of these two motives via an inferential calculus is the method least likely to damage the "real" motives of the children in question. Our choice of these two motives also reflects our sensitivity to the literature that has discussed both developmental and sex differences in terms of "social" versus "activity" orientations.

In distinguishing these two orientations, we have made judgments regarding the potential message to other children that is inherent in a given behavior—as we interpret it, as adults—and have classified behaviors as strategic in this light, proceeding as if the message we obtain from observing the behavior were the message the child intends to convey. Because of our interest in the dichotomy between activity-oriented and relationship-oriented strategies, the distinction on which we have focused in interpreting affiliative behavior is the difference between messages whose function is to explore or alter the attitudes of group members toward the entrant and messages whose sole function is to gain access for the entrant into the activity of the group.

Making inferences about the meanings of behavior has been the subject of much discussion. We have made such inferences in the present study because we believe that behaviors can be treated as if they were intended to bring about the effects that regularly follow them (compare Bowlby, 1969; Peters, 1958; Shotter, 1974). We recognize that our inferred message contents may be at variance with children's intended message contents, but we maintain that this may also be true in actual social interaction. As Mead (1934) aptly demonstrates, the way others construe a message may be the most reliable index to its meaning in any social framework. Thus, our interpretive scheme allows us to view the behavior of our subjects in the same way we view our own and others' behaviors; and this is, after all, the way behaviors acquire the strategic social values we assume they possess.

Third-Party Entry Episodes

As mentioned above, our study focuses on interactions in which one child approaches other children who are already playing and behaves as if he or she desired to join in. This interactive context, which we call the third-party entry episode, has already been the focus of previous studies.

Mallay (1935) was the first researcher to report on children's behavior during group-entry episodes. She observed five kinds of behavior in preschool children's entry attempts: looking, vocalizing, making physical contact, engaging in cooperative activity, and engaging in parallel activity. Mallay found that the last two of these five behaviors were the most likely to lead to group acceptance. Recently, Belle (1978) replicated Mallay's study, using the original descriptions of entrant behavior, but condensing "cooperative" and "parallel" activity to "related" activity and including verbalizations about the group's activity within this category. Belle also found that related activity was most likely to bring about entry into the group.

Putallaz and Gottman (1981) conducted a study in which individual children were asked to join in the play of two peers. The researchers wanted to learn something about the relationship between entry strategies and general peer popularity, as measured by a sociometric technique. Their work suggested that unpopular children tended to hover about the group prior to attempting entry, and that they also employed the entry strategies that were most related to being ignored by the group. Popular children, in contrast, showed less hovering behavior and employed the entry strategies that were most likely to result in positive responses from the group. Putallaz and Gottman noted that the behavior patterns they found in unpopular children were similar to behaviors observed in newcomers (that is, children entering a new social group for the first time).

Corsaro (1979) also studied group-entry behaviors in a sample of preschool-aged children. He examined the sequential organization of what he called "access strategies" and noted that most entry sequences in his sample began with indirect entry behaviors such as nonverbal entry, circling, producing a variant of the behavior in progress, or making a reference to friendship. Corsaro went on to observe that these strategies were the most likely to bring about immediate acceptance, but that sequences that began with one such behavior and then moved on to another indirect behavior, or to more direct entry strategies—claiming the area of an object, requesting access, questioning participants—were most likely to produce acceptance by the group. Corsaro's data are small in number and his findings are limited by the fact that all sequences consisting of two or more acts were usually successful. Still, his findings suggest the possibility that children perceive group entry as a risky situation and use indirect entry bids, in light of this perception.

One useful notion emerging from all these studies is the notion of risk in group-entry situations. Mallay's and Belle's work tells us that being direct is the best means for gaining entry into a group. Corsaro's work, however, suggests that being direct is typically preceded in actual entry sequences by being indirect—an important opening phase of entry, which may allow the child to gain feedback about group affect before directly announcing an intent to enter. Putallaz and Gottman reviewed research on newcomers to social settings (compare McGrew, 1972) and found that these children tended to hover about their peers prior to making direct approaches—another possible testimony to children's perceptions of risk. The Putallaz and Gottman study also suggests that unpopular children organize their group-entry attempts in ways that encourage their being ignored by the group. Perhaps this behavior, too, reflects use of entry styles that are less obtrusive in situations where there is a risk of rejection. In our study, then, we must pay attention to the notion of risk and examine patterns of strategy that might reflect evidence of perceived risk in third-party entry behaviors. Beyond this concern, however, we may note only that there are scant other descriptive data reporting on children's strategies for joining groups. Clearly, our study meets a need for basic information unavailable until now.

We can speculate about what will be found in this descriptive data by considering those general principles of psychological development and sex differences that have come from past efforts. Because our subjects' ages are five and seven, Sullivan's (1953) observations on the increasing salience of peer relations during middle childhood are relevant. We expect this increasing salience to be reflected in differences in entry strategies of our five- and seven-year-old subjects. The form of these differences, however, cannot be predicted precisely, since increased preoccupation with the attitudes of others toward oneself could lead either to more direct and relationally oriented entry strategies (reflecting in increased wish for relatedness) or to more indirect and activity-oriented strategies (reflecting an increased salience of rejection fears). Since planning behavior in general has been suggested as a dimension along which children develop, we should also expect our seven-year-old subjects to surpass our five-year-olds in the general level of planning displayed in third-party entry sequences.

The literature on sex differences in social behavior provides another context for expectations. We know, for instance, that girls are prone to socializing more in dyads than in larger groups, and it has also been suggested that girls are less prone than boys to adopt dominant postures when interacting with their peers (Maccoby and Jacklin, 1974). Some researchers have also suggested that girls in general may pay more attention than boys do to showing approval or agreement with others. The possibility of sex differences in affiliative styles suggests that analysis of our data according to the sex of a subject may be an important strategy for illuminating basic differences in third-party entry strategies.

We should note, too, that this study has not focused on a formal analysis either of the outcomes of third-party entry sequences or of the outcomes of specific entry bids. We considered children's responses to group feedback when we examined the sequential organization of their behavior, and we are interested in what subjects do after group feedback, not in what they did to get that feedback. (In a subsequent analysis, we shall be examining a cost-benefit model of children's third-party entry strategies, following Putallaz and Gottman, 1981).

Methods

Subjects. Twenty-four children participated in the study. Half the children were five years old (range 4:9 to 5:3) and half were seven years old (range 6:9 to 7:3). Half the children of each age were boys, and half were girls. Children participated in the study in groups of six. Each group consisted of three boys and three girls of roughly the same age (five or seven years). Each group of six children constituted a play group, upon which a separate social-behavior data base was collected (as described below). The play groups participated in a series of after-school sessions, each of which lasted for one hour. The entire series for each group consisted of twelve sessions over a period of three weeks. Subjects were drawn from the Cambridge Public School System. Each child in a given group attended a different school; no two children within any group were acquainted prior to the study.

Play-Group Sessions. Play groups met in a large playroom containing age-appropriate toys and games that were selected by a teacher-consultant, who also supervised the group sessions. The teacher remained in a small kitchen area off the playroom and did not intervene during the play-group sessions except to put out new materials and prevent physical injury or property damage. In general, the play was constant, free-flowing, and as unsupervised as possible.

All play-group sessions were recorded by a surveillance system that incorporated three cameras and six wireless microphone/transmitter units. Each child wore a small vest fitted with a wireless microphone and a transmitter. Each of the three cameras provided a different view of the playroom. We used three synchronized Sony 2800 video decks, and each deck had the capacity to record one video signal and two separate audio signals on a single video cassette; thus, three video channels (one for each camera) and six audio tracks (one for the microphone that each child wore) were recorded separately.

We were able to view the recorded behavior by simultaneously playing back the three video cassette decks. Synchronized time codes, displaying tenths of a second at the bottom of each video monitor, allowed completely synchronized viewing of all three camera angles on play-group interaction, with individual audio channels for each child. This procedure also permitted a choice of focus on any of the children or on any group of children in the playroom, without interference from the audio signals of children who were not participating in a particular interaction. We collected twelve hours of behavior records for each child in the study.

Morphological Coding. Third-party entry episodes were identified through an initial viewing of the videotapes, during which the location (by frame number) of every instance of an episode that met the criteria of a general definition was recorded. Approximately 800 group-entry approaches in all the tapes were isolated for coding purposes. Of these, some sequences were discarded. These were sequences involving approaches to the snack table (the one activity in the play-group sessions that necessarily involved all the children) and sequences in which the play-group teacher intervened (so that a child's entry into a group was partly negotiated by her). The remaining data comprised 618 sequences of social behavior.

Categories for initial coding of third-party entry sequences described the actions of a child approaching a group by reference to the action's linguistic and/or behavioral morphology. These categories were derived initially from a comprehensive system for describing observed social behavior in preschool and elementary-aged children (Forbes and Huvelle, 1978), a system that expanded on the observational taxonomy developed by Whiting (1968). Behavior categories applicable to the third-party entry situation were selected from pilot data. The system of codes was found to be adequate for describing entrant behavor, with the addition of only a single new category ("gives information–affiliative"). The categories thus created and refined bear a similarity to those developed independently by other researchers (Corsaro, 1979; Putallaz and Gottman, 1981). Code categories are presented in Table 1.

Data were coded by graduate students, who were trained in the coding system by coding tapes from pilot play-group sessions. Coders were instructed to assign a separate behavior code for each "turn" of behavior on the part of entrants. A "turn" was defined (after Garvey, 1974) as an utterance or a behavior of the entrant child that was not interrupted by an utterance or a behavior of a

Table 1. Categories for Morphological Coding of Children's Third-Party Entry Bids

01 *Approaches.* Child places self near the group, without engaging group members in conversation and without joining in.
02 *Joins.* Child joins in the activity of the group, without verbalization codeable in other category.
03 *Asks to join.* Child directly requests permission to join in the activity of the group.
04 *Intrudes/Barges in.* Child enters the activity of the group in a manner that requires others to change physical position, abandon materials, or alter the nature of their activity; code when the physical actions of the entrant child bring about these consequences.
05 *Pleads.* Child makes request for group entry with the use of polite words or with pleading tone of voice.
06 *Appeals to norms.* Child makes reference to a social rule or norm that requires the group members to allow him or her to join in the activity.
07 *Suggests role for self in group activity.* Child suggests actions which he or she could perform that would be related to the group play.
08 *Suggests new activity.* Child suggests new activity for self and members of the group.
09 *Displays.* Child makes reference to his or her own characteristics, possessions, or activity in a positive comment.
10 *Asserts superiority.* Child makes a comparative statement in which his or her characteristics are compared with those of a member of the group, in a manner that denigrates the other and/or elevates self.
11 *Criticizes.* Child makes a statement about others' abilities or characteristics that is negative, without element of comparison to self.
12 *Flatters.* Child makes reference to others' characteristics, possessions, or activity in a positive comment.
13 *Seeks Information–Instrumental.* Child asks factual question of group member that is unrelated to the activity of the group or to the characteristics of a group member.
14 *Seeks Information–Affiliative.* Child asks questions of group member regarding member's characteristics of group's activity.

group member. When a turn of behavior could be coded in two or more of the categories, coders were instructed to choose the more complex or more socially forceful of the behavior codes in question (codes were ranked by number along this dimension). Responses of group members to behaviors of entrants were coded as negative, positive, or unclear, according to the valance members expressed with respect to entrants' presence and/or participation in group conversation or activity.

Reliability was assessed by independent double-coding of 100 entry sequences selected at random from the data corpus. An overall percentage agreement of .68 was obtained. To assess reliability, in light of the complexity of the coding system, a Cohen-weighted Kappa was calculated, with disagreement between morphologically similar categories weighted as one-half agreement and disagreement between dissimilar categories weighted as total disagreement. This statistic, which also discounts for probability of chance coder agreement, was .82.

Sequential Coding. Third-party entry behaviors coded in the morphological-description language were recoded for the sequential analysis. The sequential meaning of a given entry behavior could vary, depending on its location in the sequence. The recoding process therefore augmented information about the surface structure of the behavior (as coded in the morphological language) with information about its relationship to the sequence as a whole. Thus, initial behaviors in an entry sequence were coded differently from later behaviors in the sequence, since these opening moves were made without the benefit of group feedback about its receptivity to the entrant. Later moves in the entry sequence were evaluated in terms of their relationships with the interactions that preceded them. The preceding behaviors of the entrants themselves, as well as the response of group members to these preceding behaviors, were considered in the coding of these midgame strategies.

Codes for opening moves in an entry sequence were designed to distinguish both the motivational orientation of the opening bid and the strategic value of the bid with respect to its inferred motivational orientation. In all, seven categories of opening moves were distinguished; these categories and their definitions appear in Table 2. Entrants opening moves were classified as relationally oriented strategies when they involved acknowledging the entrants' role as an outsider. Entrants' suggestions of roles for themselves in the group's activity, in contrast, were coded as activity-oriented moves, since such action on an entrant's part addresses only the relationship between the entrant and the group activity. As outlined in Table 2, relationally oriented opening moves were classified into four types, each of which has a somewhat different implication for the status of the entrant with respect to the group, and activity-oriented moves were classified into three types, which reflect different implications regarding the relationship between activity and entrant.

Whenever possible, the initial behavior of an entrant child was assigned to an opening-move category solely on the basis of its surface structure.

Table 2. Codes for Opening Moves in Children's Third-Party Entry Sequences

Activity Orientation (A)

A1. *Simple entry.* Child begins interaction with the group by joining in the activity or directly making a suggestion for activity. Approaching the group is also coded as a simple activity-oriented approach when this behavior is followed by joining the activity.

A2. *Surveillance.* Child begins interaction with the group by approaching or seeking affiliative information and then responds to group feedback with a midgame move in the activity orientation.

A3. *Forced entry.* Child begins interaction by barging into group activity or by appealing to norms that dictate admission to group activity.

Relational Orientation (R)

R1. *Simple entry.* Child begins interaction by asking permission to join in group activity. "Approach" is also coded as a simple relational entry when it is followed by asking to join or by a suggestion for self's role in group activity (in cases of positive feedback) or by "displaying" or "criticizing" (in cases of negative feedback).

R2. *Surveillance.* "Seeks information–instrumental," when followed by a relational midgame move, is coded as surveillance. All cases of "gives information–affiliative" are coded as surveillance. "Seeks information–affiliative" is coded as surveillance when it is the only entry bid in an episode, or when it is followed by a relational midgame move. Approaches are coded as surveillance in the relational mode when they are followed by another form of relational surveillance.

R3. *Subdominance.* Child begins interaction with flattery of group member or with plea for entry into group's activity.

R4. *Forced entry.* Child begins interaction with "displays," "asserts superiority," or "criticizes."

When the surface structure of the initial bid did not allow for such assignment, the feedback to the opening move and the entrant's behavior following this feedback were considered as classifying the opening move retrospectively.

Classification of midgame moves within the dimensions of relational and activity orientation was intended to distinguish the various ways in which a child could respond to either positive or negative feedback. The concept of "enablement" was central to this classificatory scheme: Categories in the relational midgame move taxonomy distinguish modes of strategic action that enable a positive status with respect to the group in the face of group resistance (negative feedback), as well as modes of strategic action that build positive group status upon enablement from the group (positive feedback); categories in the activity-oriented midgame taxonomy distinguish modes of strategic action for gaining access to group activity in the face of enabling (positive) or disabling (negative) feedback from the group. Classification of midgame moves relied on a system of ten categories. These categories and their definitions appear in Table 3.

In all cases, the classification of midgame moves relied on information about immediately preceding behavior and about the group response to this behavior. Classification of opening as well as midgame moves began in a heuristic fashion, with the sequential codes brought into play for specific instances of morphologically coded entry sequences (see the definitions provided in Tables 2 and 3). Reliability in the heuristic coding phase was computed for 75 sequences comprising a total of 122 behaviors. Percentage agreement in this assessment was .92. The result of this coding process, however, is a decision tree, which codes entry behaviors on an algorithmic basis. (While this decision tree is too complex to be reproduced here, it is available upon request.) Application of the decision tree to the morphologically coded data resulted in the recoding of 561 of the 618 third-party entry sequences. The remaining 57 sequences, which could not be accommodated by the decision tree, were eliminated from the sequential analysis.

Results

Recoding of the third-party entry data for sequential analysis yielded a total of 561 sequences, which included a total of 561 opening moves and 494

Table 3. Midgame Moves in Children's Third-Party Entry Sequences

Activity Orientation (A)

A4. *Ignore and proceed.* In response to negative feedback, child proceeds behaviorally as if this feedback were not obtained. This includes doing a second bid codeable as "simple entry" after a first bid coded "simple entry"; doing a second bid codeable as "forced entry" following a first bid coded "forced entry"; and doing a second bid codeable as "simple entry" following a first bid of surveillance.

A5. *De-escalation.* In response to negative feedback, a child who began the entry interaction with a "forced entry" bid does a second bid codeable as a "simple entry" or as a "surveillance."

A6. *Escalation.* In response to negative feedback, a child who began a sequence with a "simple entry" or a "surveillance" does a second bid codeable as a "forced entry."

A7. *Simple follow-up.* Following positive feedback from the group to an initial entry bid, entrant does second bid codeable as a "simple" or "surveillance" opening move.

A8. *Activity* coup d'état. Following positive feedback to an activity move, subject suggests a new activity.

Relational Orientation (R)

R5. *Ignore and proceed.* Following negative feedback to a relational move, subject repeats that bid or does bid codeable as "barges," "joins," or "radical suggestion."

R6. *Repair.* Following negative feedback to any move, subject does bid coded as "seeks information–affiliative," "gives information–affiliative," or "asks to join," or subject does bid codeable as a "subdominant" relational move.

R7. *Face saving.* Following negative feedback to any move, subject makes second bid coded as "display" or "criticize." Following negative feedback to a relational move, subject makes bid coded as "appeals to norms."

R8. *Simple follow-up.* Following positive feedback to a relational move, subject makes a second move codeable as a "simple," "surveillance," or "subdominant" move.

R9. *Social* coup d'état. Following positive feedback to a relational move, subject makes a second move codeable as a "forced" relational move or makes a suggestion for new activity.

midgame moves. Of the total sequences, 256 were episodes of only one act (sequences where the child achieved entry or gave up after one bid); 152 were sequences of two acts; and 153 were sequences of three acts. No differences in the length of sequences for the five- and seven-year-old age groups were apparent, nor were differences in length of sequence associated with sex of subject.

Our first investigation of the data focused on functional aspects of children's third-party entry attempts. We began this phase by examining the distribution of relationally oriented entry bids and activity-oriented entry bids across the course of the play-group sessions. This analysis compared data from the first six sessions with data from the last six. Given the "newcomer" notion, we expected initially unfamiliar subjects to show greater orientation toward joining group activity than toward establishing a social relationship with group members, since the latter orientation involves increased social risk. We also expected subjects to show increased orientation to relational issues in their entry attempts as they came to know other group members during the last six sessions, when the risk of any given entry attempt would be decreased because of greater experience with the others.

Our results show that relational orientation was predominant for about half the subjects in the first six sessions and for two-thirds of subjects in the last six sessions. A chi-square analysis of this pattern does not uphold our prediction of absolute predominance for activity versus relational strategies in the first six versus the last six group sessions ($x^2 = 1.36 p \leq .25$). Nevertheless, a sign test for the predicted direction of change does yield significance ($p \leq .02$), with eighteen of the twenty-four subjects increasing relational orientation from the first six sessions to the last six.

Our next analysis looked for age and sex differences in the children's use of activity and relational bids. In line with our introductory remarks, we expected older children to show a greater tendency in all sessions to use strategies with relational orientations and that girls would show a greater tendency to relational orientation than boys would. We also tested for newcomer effects in sequences occurring in the first six play-group sessions versus the last six, with the expectation that our general findings in this respect might vary across dimensions of age and sex. All our analyses relied on the Fisher Exact Probability Test of the proportions of the above behaviors from a child's total entry bids, split at the median for all subjects.

Contrary to our expectations, no significant age or sex differences were found in overall use of activity or relational strategies. When data from the first and the last six play-group sessions were analyzed separately, however, we found an age effect in the first six sessions. Five-year-old children showed less use of relational bids than did seven-year-olds. The Fisher Exact Probability Test showed this difference to be significant at $p \leq .02$.

The second phase of our analysis examined the structural features of the third-party entry episodes. In this phase, we investigated general differences in sophistication of sequential organization, with the expectation that the seven-year-olds would show more sophistication than the five-year-olds would. In particular, we examined the distribution of "ignore and proceed" as a response to negative feedback. Results indicated that our expectations in this respect were confirmed. A median-split Fisher Exact Test for total proportions of "ignore and proceed"—irrespective of orientation—indicated a significant effect for age ($p \le .025$), with five-year-old subjects showing much more of this pattern than did seven-year-olds. In a second analysis, we examined the cases where "ignore and proceed" was repeated within a single episode. While the overall number of these sequences is too low for statistical evaluation, the results are rather dramatic in simple numbers: Twenty-three cases of repeated ignore-and-proceed moves were located in the data; of these, eighteen were found in the records of five-year-old subjects. Thus, developmental differences in the manifestation of unsophisticated planning behavior are clearly apparent in our data.

A third analysis sought to examine interactions between the structure of third-party entry sequences and the motivations of the sequences. We examined the proportions of ignore-and-proceed moves separately in this analysis for sequences with activity orientations and sequences with relational orientations. It was expected that a sex-by-age-by-sequence–type of interaction would obtain in this analysis—that is, that girls' greater orientation to social aspects of interactions would produce earlier structural sophistication in relationally oriented sequences. A general increase in the salience of peer relations was expected to eliminate this difference in the older children. These expectations were upheld. Girls showed an overall lesser tendency to "ignore and proceed" in the relational mode than they did in the activity mode. Ten of twelve female subjects showed a smaller proportion of ignore-and-proceed behavior in the relational mode than in the activity mode, while boys were evenly split in this respect (Fisher Exact $p \le .002$). Furthermore, while girls were significantly less prone than boys to "ignore and proceed" in the relational mode at age five ($p \le .05$), boys showed greater decreases than girls did in this tendency from age five to age seven ($p \le .05$), such that there were no differences between boys and girls in this respect at age seven. In parallel analysis of "ignore and proceed" in the activity mode, no similar patterns were detected.

Finally, we investigated qualitative differences among the moves children made in their attempts to enter play groups. Three forms of interactive plans were investigated. First, we looked at the propensity to adopt a "forceful" status with respect to the group in the opening move of a third-party entry episode. In the relational mode, this strategy was identified as beginning a sequence by displaying one's own qualities, asserting superiority over group members, or criticizing members of the group. In the activity-oriented mode, a "forceful" opening move meant barging into the group activity or appealing to playroom norms which mandate acceptance. Analysis of patterns of "forced" opening moves suggests that the plan of beginning a relational sequence with a position of "force" was used significantly more by boys than by girls at both ages ($p \le .025$). No patterns in the use of "forceful" openings were discovered in the analysis of activity-oriented sequences.

In a second analysis, we examined children's use of "pressure" in response to negative feedback by focusing on the midgame move of "escalation" in the activity mode and on the move of "face saving" in the relational mode. Both of these strategies were viewed as means by which a child could apply "pressure" in service of the entry goal when meeting resistance from the group (see Table 3 for complete definitions of these moves). Analysis of patterns in these midgame moves showed a significant sex difference in the use of "face saving," with boys at both ages showing a greater propensity to "save face" than girls did. No significant patterns were discovered in the use of "escalation" during activity-oriented sequences.

In a third descriptive analysis, we examined interactive plans involving "accommodation" to the group following negative feedback. In the relational mode, this strategy involved asking neutral questions of group members, making neutral comments about oneself, or asking permission to join the group; in the activity mode, this strategy was scored when a child retreated from a "forced" opening move to a less forceful move (see Tables 2 and 3). Because there were not enough of these two types of midgame moves for separate analysis, they were combined for exploratory purposes. Results of this analysis suggest an interaction between sex and age in the use of plans that call for accommodating to a group in the face of negative feedback. No differences existed at age five, but boys decreased significantly in the use of this plan between ages five and seven, while girls remained at roughly static levels ($p \le .05$), such that girls were more prone than boys were to employ this strategy by age seven ($p \le .05$).

Discussion

This study has sought to document developmental and sex-linked differences in children's planning behavior, as manifested in the sequential organization of their actions when they attempt to enter play groups. Our interest in planning behavior led us to create a sequential-code language for describing the social interactions we observed. We have emphasized structural as well as functional aspects of our social-behavior sequences, since goals and strategies are both important dimensions of individual planning. Accordingly, we hoped to learn about differences in the apparent motives with which children approached playmates and sought group admission and to focus on the general level of behavioral organization during such episodes. Finally, because of the inseparability of structure from function as dimension for discussing development, we sought information about their interplay in our data.

The results of our efforts appear quite interesting. First, we have documented differences in the apparent motives that bring children to approach playmates and seek group entry over the course of an acquaintanceship process. When first encountering one another, the children in our sample were less prone to approach peers with behaviors that make an issue of social status than they were after a period of getting to know each other. Negotiation of social status during group-entry occasions increased as acquaintanceship grew. Perhaps, as past studies suggest, our "newcomers" perceived group entry initially as a risky social situation. As knowledge about the others increased, they were more willing to engage in entry attempts in which social status was explicitly an issue. Our inability to find general age or sex effects in motivation during third-party entry situations may suggest that the distinction between social orientation and action orientation was too global for characterizing differences between the sexes or for describing the course of social development over age; the interaction between age and early and later play-group sessions in patterns of social and activity motivation may suggest a more detailed descriptive alternative. Our five-year-olds pursued relational issues far less often in the opening play-group sessions than did our seven-year-olds, a difference that disappeared in the later sessions. Within a "newcomer" framework, this may suggest that five-year-olds are more sensitive to the riskiness of group entry among strangers than are seven-year-olds—perhaps because, as Corsaro suggests, this social episode is, indeed, more risky for the younger children. (In fact, frequency of active group rejection for our five-year-olds was about .16 in early sessions, as compared to .06 for seven-year-olds.) We suggest, alternatively, that our seven-year-old subjects were concerned enough with social-relatedness issues that they began to negotiate them immediately, despite the interpersonal risk. Clearly, more work on this issue is required.

Our findings regarding general structural features of behavioral organization in third-party entry episodes compare well with typical accounts of development. We would expect five-year-olds to be less able than seven-year-olds to respond to negative feedback from others in a strategic fashion, since the ability to behave cybernetically with respect to one's environment is a continuum along which, theoretically, development should be charted. The incidence of repeated ignore-and-proceed moves in the five-year-old subjects underscores the notion that five-year-olds are less responsive than seven-year-olds to the contingencies of the social environment. We should note, however, that it may be unwise to impute ineptness on the basis of finding that a child ignores feedback from others in a social situation like that of third-party entry. Corsaro finds that children are very likely to gain admission to a group if they simply continue to do anything into a second or third round of interaction. We should also note in this context that the overall rate for gaining eventual access to the group activity was not different for our five- and seven-year-old children (about 35 percent in both cases).

Our findings regarding the interaction between structure and function are, perhaps, most interesting. We seem to have evidence for earlier development in girls of the ability to plan behavior in situations where social relationships are being negotiated during a bid for group acceptance. It also seems that boys tend to catch up in this area between the ages of five and seven, as social development makes relations with peers an increasingly salient issue. This finding supports past results both on sex differences and on general social development while integrating the two areas. It appears that girls may be oriented earlier to social aspects of interactions, such that they acquire competencies in this area earlier; but it also seems true that a general pattern of increasingly social orientation of both sexes over age (compare Sullivan, 1953) mitigates this difference by age seven.

Our inability to find age or sex differences in activity-oriented planning behavior brings up the caveat we have already issued. Perhaps our measure of "ignore and proceed" is an inappropriate index for measuring planning-behavior changes in our subjects' age range. If the ignore-and-proceed strategy is a simple but effective means of gaining entry to the group, it may well be that our five-year-old children already use it because of its simplicity, while our seven-year-old children continue to employ it because of its effectiveness. It should be remembered that our definition of activity-oriented sequences involved attention to activity access, rather than to social relations. Perhaps an activity goal can be pursued effectively without attention to negative feedback from group members, since it may be their activity that is of interest, not their attitude toward the entrant.

Our exploratory analysis of some qualitative categories of plans for third-party entry also provides suggestions about this phenomenon. In the relational mode, "forceful" opening moves were used more by boys than by girls at both ages. Similarly, we noted that face saving in response to negative feedback was more prevalent in the relational mode among boys of both ages. These two findings, especially considered together, strongly suggest that the boys were more prone to be assertive about their status with peers in group-entry situations. In terms of "plans" for group entry, it would seem that, for our male subjects, a goal of attaining positive status in the group may have taken precedence over a goal of gaining acceptance by the group.

This issue is elaborated by our findings on accommodation to others in response to negative feedback. We noted that boys and girls were initially not different with respect to this behavior, but that boys decreased significantly in this pattern from age five to age seven, such that girls accommodated significantly more than boys by age seven. It appears that the boys were "unlearning" the plan of making accommodations to group members in the face of negative feedback, while the girls were maintaining this behavior at a level that placed them ahead of the boys by age seven. Since accommodation to the group would be a strategy aimed at acceptance by the group (but not at attaining status with respect to the group), this finding reinforces the speculations we offer above. These findings are consistent with past reports of heightened propensities for dominance among boys (Maccoby and Jacklin, 1974; Whiting and Edwards, 1973). Our findings also suggest, however, that boys may employ dominant postures in some situations purely for the sake of status elevations, rather than simply in the pursuit of instrumental objectives (for example, "liberating" a play material from a peer).

Conclusions

In this chapter, we have suggested one approach to the analysis of structure and function in children's social behavior, an approach that permits attention to the development of planning behavior as a cybernetic phenomenon in the individual child. Our investigation suggests that the relationship between structure and function is an important consideration for researchers studying social behavior and development, and we have demonstrated the value of engaging in a process of careful inference about children's motives, based on our observation of the strategies they employ during social interaction. The notion that planning is an important dimension for charting the development of social skill has been supported by our findings. The examination of sequential ordering in the actions of individuals who are construed as employing strategies in continuing pursuit of an underlying goal has helped us offer some preliminary insight into the development of structure in behavior. In related work, we are expanding the use of the planning model by making separate examinations of the assessed social-cognitive skills of our subject children and by documenting relationships between these skills that may underlie planning and the behavioral order characteristic of plans in action.

Throughout the study, we have been frustrated in our sequential analysis by the lack of a data base large enough to allow for fine attention to other important parameters of the group-entry situation, particularly the identities of the children approached and the nature of their activity at the time of approach. These two variables, as well as others the reader can no doubt imagine, must play an important role in shaping the planning process. As anyone who has attempted to gather social-behavior data knows, however, the costs of accumulating behavior records and coding them for analysis can become quite unwieldy, and the efforts of individual investigators must be limited, except in the most fortuitous circumstances. Accordingly, we appeal to fellow investigators for collaboration in creating a coding scheme that can be shared across projects and permit integration of the data necessary to mount truly detailed analyses of social-behavior patterns. Through such an effort, psychology may attain some real understanding of how children form and execute plans in the social world.

References

Bakeman, R., and Brownlee, J. "The Strategic Use of Parallel Play: A Sequential Analysis." *Child Development,* 1980, *51,* 873–878.

Bates, E. *Language and Context: The Acquisition of Pragmatics.* New York: Academic Press, 1976.

Belle, D. "The Preschool Child's Techniques for Entering Social Groups." Unpublished doctoral dissertation, Graduate School of Education, Harvard University, 1978.

Bowlby, J. *Attachment and Loss.* Vol. 1. *Attachment.* New York: Basic Books, 1969.

Corsaro, W. "'We're Friends, Right?': Children's Use of Access Rituals in a Nursery School." *Language in Society,* 1979, *8* (3), 315–336.
Dodge, K. A. "Social Cognition and Children's Aggressive Behavior." *Child Development,* 1980, *51,* 162–170.
Dore, J. "Children's Illocutionary Acts." In R. Freedle (Ed.), *Discourse Production and Comprehension.* Vol. 1. Norwood, N.J.: Ablex, 1977.
Forbes, D., and Huvelle, N. *The Naturalistic Observation Schedule: A System for Coding Social Behavior in Preschool.* Unpublished manuscript, Research Institute for Educational Problems, Cambridge, Mass., 1978.
Forbes, D., and Lubin, D. *Overview of Results from the First Three Years of the Peer Interaction Project.* Section II: *The Cognitive Component.* Unpublished manuscript, Harvard University, 1981.
Garvey, C. "Some Properties of Social Play." In J. S. Bruner, A. Jolly, and K. Sylva (Eds.), *Play—Its Role in Development and Evolution.* New York: Basic Books, 1974.
Garvey, C. "Requests and Responses in Children's Speech." *Journal of Child Language,* 1975, *2,* 41–63.
Gottman, J. "Detecting Cyclicity in Social Interaction." *Psychological Bulletin,* 1979, *86,* 338–348.
Haslett, B. "'I'll Give You a Knuckle Sandwich': Preschoolers' Resolution of Conflict." Paper presented at Speech Communication Association meetings, November 1980.
Kaplan, B. "Rationality and Irrationality in Development: Strife of Systems." Heinz Weaver Memorial Lecture, Clark University, Worcester, Mass., October 9, 1974.
Klahr, D., and Robinson, M. "Formal Assessment of Problem-Solving and Planning Processes in Preschool Children." *Cognitive Psychology,* 1981, *13,* 113–147.
Lakoff, R. "The Logic of Politeness; Or, Minding Your P's and Q's." In C. Corum, T. C. Smith-Stark, and A. Weiser (Eds.), *Papers from the Ninth Regional Meeting, Chicago Linguistic Society.* Chicago: Chicago Linguistic Society, 1973.
Maccoby, E., and Jacklin, C. *The Psychology of Sex Differences.* Stanford, Calif.: Stanford University Press, 1974.
McGrew, W. C. *An Ethological Study of Children's Behavior.* New York: Academic Press, 1972.
Mallay, H. "A Study of Some of the Techniques Underlying the Establishment of Successful Social Contacts at the Preschool Level." *Journal of Genetic Psychology,* 1935, *47,* 431–457.
Mead, G. H. *Mind, Self and Society.* Chicago: University of Chicago Press, 1934.
Nelson, K., and Gruendel, J. M. "At Morning It's Lunchtime: A Scriptal View of Children's Dialogues." *Discourse Processes,* 1979, *2,* 73–94.
Peters, R. S. *The Concept of Motivation.* London: Routledge & Kegan Paul, 1958.
Putallaz, M., and Gottman, J. "An Interactional Model of Children's Entry into Peer Groups." *Child Development,* 1981, *52,* 986–994.
Shotter, J. "The Development of Personal Powers." In M. P. M. Richards (Ed.), *The Integration of a Child into a Social World.* London: Cambridge University Press, 1974.
Siegler, R. S. "Developmental Sequences Within and Between Concepts." *Monographs of the Society for Research in Child Development,* 1981, *46* (2), Serial no. 189.
Sullivan, H. S. *The Interpersonal Theory of Psychiatry.* New York: Norton, 1953.
Whiting, B. *A Transcultural Code for the Study of Social Behavior.* Unpublished paper, Laboratory of Human Development, Harvard University, 1968.
Whiting, B., and Edwards, C. "A Cross-Cultural Analysis of Sex Differences in the Behavior of Children Aged 3 to 11." *Journal of Social Psychology,* 1973, *91,* 171–188.

David L. Forbes is research associate at the Laboratory of Human Development, Harvard Graduate School of Education. He is also director of the Peer Interaction Project at the Harvard Graduate School of Education.

Mary Maxwell Katz is lecturer and senior research coordinator at the Laboratory of Human Development, Harvard Graduate School of Education.

Barry Paul is a doctoral candidate in the psychology department at Brandeis University.

David Lubin is research associate at the Laboratory of Human Development, Harvard Graduate School of Education.

Communication with both caregivers and peers about pretend role enactments precedes the appearance of social role play in the third year of life.

Communication and the Development of Social Role Play

Catherine Garvey

The tendency of young children to reproduce, voluntarily and in their own manner, the familiar activities of their elders has been observed in diverse cultures. This tendency appears before children are old enough to execute these behaviors productively and often before there is any attempt by adults to shape or instruct children in efficient execution of the behaviors—stringing shells for a necklace, molding a clay pot, serving a meal, using a telephone, and so forth. Adults usually find these childish imitations intelligible and amusing. At the basic level of childish attempts to enact adult behavior, pretend role play may be as important to children's survival as are the physiological characteristics of immaturity that Lorenz viewed as innate releasing mechanisms of affectional and nurturant behavior by adults. From this basic level, which is widely tolerated if not encouraged by adults, many parents go on to assist children actively in the elaboration of adult-role enactment in a nonliteral key. Where pretend play is valued, these enactments may be selectively shaped by adults along culturally accepted lines. Thus, even before cooperative role play in the peer setting is common, most children have acquired a repertoire of conventional behaviors for role enactments, as well as some of the communicative techniques by which such play can be shared with others.

The research reported in this chapter was supported by a grant from the Spencer Foundation.

How and when are the conventions and the skills required for social role play acquired? Toddlers, although they engage in short bouts of interactive play and can recognize and copy partner's nonliteral acts, have not been observed to carry out joint enactments of adultlike behavior. Young two-year-olds have begun to handle dolls and replicas in conventionally appropriate ways in nonsocial play. It is not known, however, when the two essential elements of social-role play—the adoption or assignments of roles and the incorporation of a partner into a pretend action line—converge to produce mature peer play. This issue is the focus of this chapter.

Pretend play, and especially role play, depends on conventional procedures for transposing systems of social meaning and for operating on these domains in intelligible ways. In the mature social play of four-year-old children, the actual setting, objects, persons, and events are transformed and integrated into a performance. The production is effected by acting out and by talk that functions not only to create the transformations and indicate the action but also to direct the interactions of the participants. Communications "in role" and communications about the playing alternate; both types of communications are vital to the play. They are equally important to observers who would understand this common activity of childhood as an accomplishment in its own right or to those who would infer from play behavior children's level of competence in interaction, their knowledge of social structures, or their cognitive development in some other domain (for example, perspectivism, or extent of abstraction of social role systems).

Before proceeding to discuss the social and communicational aspects of role play, let us note that contemporary work whose primary focus is on individual cognitive development has outlined the cognitive constraints on important changes in play that take place during the first three years of life. This work has also delineated the structural components of pretend play in reference to the cognitive achievements that may be inferred from observation of play behavior. These components, discussed by Fein (1981), are decontextualization, object substitution, sequential combination of actions, and self-other relations.

Using these categories, we may describe the changing cognitive abilities of children, as they are reflected in observed changes in play. *Decontextualization* refers to decreasing dependence on perceptible context or setting. With the emergence of representation, actions and events can be displaced from their immediate contexts and from their normal antecedents and goals. A child can then pretend to eat, even though he is not hungry, or sleep, even when not tired. *Object substitution* refers to increasing freedom from the demand features of object properties and object functions, as concepts come to exert more control over behavior. A hand or a block can serve as an iron if a child formulates the intention of pretending to iron a dress. *Sequential combination* refers to increasing linkage and integration of discrete actions to reproduce the sense, if not the precise order and detail, of some procedure or event complex.

A baby doll is not only given a bottle but is also burped, fed again, burped again, and laid down to sleep. Furthermore, the constituent steps of a procedure come to be elaborated, so that burping, for example, can be done quite realistically. *Self-other relations* reflect children's increasing capacity to discriminate and objectify the characteristics and relationships of themselves and others; this capacity includes the ability to use self and others to depict these relationships in play.

These components of pretend play are linked together by the operation of planning—that is, conceiving of an outcome or a final configuration of affairs and subsequently working toward that end. The preconceived outcome or state of affairs takes precedence over immediate sensory perceptions in guiding action with objects and in shaping the child's orientation toward and reaction to others. Huttenlocher and Higgins (1978) proposed that an advance announcement of a transformation, or a verbal expression of a concept in the absence of a physical object that the expression selects, should be criteria for inferring a symbolic operation on the part of very young children. Similarly, Winner and others (1979) proposed that renaming serves as an index of a covert metaphoric operation, provided that the child also indicates knowledge of the real identity or conventional function of an object (that is, the child is not confused or in error). The expression of plans for pretending or intended pretend transformations may be criteria for investigators who are concerned with children's symbolic capability or with special forms of nonliteral operations; the verbalization of a plan or a transformation also helps children themselves to conduct the play activity.

While the primarily cognitive focus of past research has proved fruitful in illuminating the structure of play-related skills, we would argue that the developmental history of role play is tied more closely than has been thought to interpersonal experiences. Children learn to conduct such play, first with adult support or even explicit training or modeling, and then with age-mates, whose function grows during the third year of life from child partner to include role-play partner as well. As play behavior becomes more and more conventional, actions come to signify arbitrary systems of meaning that are beyond (and sometimes in conflict with) the intrinsic properties of objects. This process is intricately linked with the social use of language to interpret, confirm, and place in conventional context the significance of an object or a gesture. Public announcement of a plan or an intentional event provides others who are present an opportunity to acknowledge the intelligibility of the child's formulated intention. It also permits others to assist in the extension or modification of the plan, thus encoding for the first time a plan or a transformation that the child himself may not have foreseen clearly. It is precisely such communication about pretending that parents offer to young children. Individual activity is thus subject to support and shaping by others at the very beginning of pretend play—as, for example, when a parent responds to a child's utterance, "Sleep," and the child's accompanying action of laying a doll on a sofa, by saying,

"Oh, Baby's tired. You're gonna put her in for her nap?" That parents do provide such support, and that such assistance changes over time with the child's capabilities, is indicated by recent work (Kavanaugh, Whittington, and Cerbone, 1981; Sachs, in press). How role play is achieved by young peers, however, and what the contribution of peer interaction might be to the onset of role play are still unknown factors.

In this chapter, we shall discuss recent reports and our own observations of child–adult and child–child interactions. The development of role play will be outlined, with particular emphasis on the functions of partners and their communications. The achievement of reciprocal role play with peers is a relatively late accomplishment. It incorporates the above-mentioned components of pretend play, integrated by and subservient to a plan and dependent on communication with partners. We shall first examine the mature forms of such play and then suggest the steps in its development.

Our description draws on a cross-sectional sample of dyadic peer interactions videotaped in a laboratory playroom. The procedures have been described elsewhere for previously acquainted dyads (Garvey and Berndt, 1977) and for those meeting in the playroom for the first time (Lieberman, 1977). Together, more than eighty dyads were observed. Both same- and mixed-sex dyads were included, and pairings were made of children who were approximately the same age. The youngest dyads were 2:10–3:3; the oldest, 4:7–5:7. Toys conducive to role play (for example, an ironing board, a baby doll, a cradle) and toys less apparently suggestive of role-related activity (for example, blocks, a stuffed snake) were provided.

Three aspects of role play are of primary interest—the content, the enactment techniques, and the regulation techniques. The enactment techniques include communication "in role"; the production and regulation techniques include communications about the play and occur prior to, during, and following the pretend episodes.

Content Categories in Children's Role Play

The content of role play can be described according to the domain from which the roles and role relationships are derived and in terms of the themes and story lines that guide the actions of the characters. A "taxonomy" of role types distinguishes functional, relational or family, occupational, and fantasy roles. Functional roles are those based on performance of an activity. They may be assigned and adopted without further person identification. For example, a child may say, "I'm the cook" and pretend to prepare supper and serve a partner, without claiming the role of Mother or Big Sister. Relational roles are those derived from stable interpersonal relationships—Mother, Father, Child, Sister, Wife, and relevant others such as Friend or Pet. (In this chapter, relational role titles will be capitalized, except when they occur in direct quotations.) Occupational roles are those impersonal identities derived solely from the work—for example, dentist, teacher, and fireman. Functional and occupational roles generally imply complementary person functions—for example, driver and passenger or teacher and pupil. The consistent and often obligatory execution of functional roles, of course, is a substantive part of other roles; as one three-year-old said to his girl partner, "You're the mommy—cook." Certain functional roles are prohibited to some persons—for example, "Daddies don't cook." Fantasy roles, which may be further distinguished by their sources in stories, folklore, television or pure or impure imagination, are characters with whom the child has had no interpersonal experience—Hansel and Gretel, Big Bird, Superman, and Mr. Poop, for example.

All these roles rest on abstract concepts of person functions, relationships, and characteristics, rather than on direct identification with a particular real person. Actual persons, when present, are referred to and addressed appropriately. For example, the partner's real mother is called correctly, "Mrs. Porter," and the nursery school teacher is called "Mrs. Black." Actual persons may also be referred to by role title: "My teacher is having her coffee." Moreover, young children may enact a telephone conversation, announcing, "I'm gonna call my daddy." No child in our sample, however, ever adopted or assigned such an actual individual identity; that is, a child usually says to a partner, "I'll be the mommy." If the child says to the partner, "I'll be your mommy," the child is referring the the Mommy of the imaginary Baby or Child whom the partner is to become, not to the real partner's veritable mother. Just as, in this literature, one refers to the Child, so do children in role play refer to the Baby, the doctor, or the Daddy. Persons in role play are thus type-categorized, although some of their features may be influenced by the child's personal experiences with familiar individuals.

For relational roles, at least one role complement is obligatory, and the nuclear family is often represented. The roles seem to be conceptualized as points in a relationship, which do not occur in isolation. No child in our sample occupied a relational role without using at least a doll as a role counterpart. Few fantasy figures were ever portrayed as solitary, and occupations roles were usually complemented as well—for example, doctors partnered by patients, Superman by Batman or Robin, a cowboy by a cowgirl.

Among four-year-olds, story lines and themes may be either predominantly realistic (that is, following, although often quite sketchily, a set of procedures for some event such as taking a vacation) or they may be primarily fantastic (for example, escaping or overwhelming a dreaded monster). Play episodes may also be a combination of the two. The diversity of themes and story lines increases with age, and this, again, reflects to some extent children's own experiences with actual social events, with television, with stories, and probably with the play of other children. The most widely observed theme, and the first to appear in social role play, is the domestic theme, in which the personas of the primary relational roles carry out the familiar procedures of childcare and housework.

Much-needed longitudinal studies of role play would probably show increasing breadth and depth of children's awareness of family structure and the functions of family members. Two considerations, however, would militate against a too-literal interpretation of such play as an index to knowledge of social arrangements and procedures. The first is the frequent blending of fantasy and realistic themes; the second is the stereotyping and the schematicization of pretend themes. Familiar or standard components in a theme may be only fleetingly suggested or may be skipped altogether in the enactment, while other components may be repetitively enacted and elaborated—cups and cups and cups of tea are poured, sugared, stirred, and drunk, for example. Repetition is not limited to the play of younger children.

An example from an older dyad will illustrate the mixture of realistic and fantasy themes, as well as the repetition, foreshortening, and allusiveness of thematic components. First, a Husband brings home his earnings to the Wife. He is quite proud, and she is grateful and delighted. She then gives him her earned money, and he is similarly touched: "Oh, thank you, honey." He suggests that they can now take a vacation "at a beautiful hotel in the only favorite place, Puerto Rico." They start to leave immediately (without packing) and she drives off while he flies down. Having arrived in Puerto Rico, they are on a beach, where the Husband sees a monster and kills it to protect his Wife. She decides to drive back to Baltimore, and he reminds her that she must wait for him "'cause I'm your husband, honey." Back home (no travelling enacted on his part), he discovers a fire in the living room. He dons a fireman's hat and puts out the blaze with a fire hose (actually, a stuffed snake). The Wife spots another and yet another fire. He rushes around to the different rooms, putting out the fires and reassuring his Wife, until it appears that the fire is also in the sky and might even "kill God." The firehose-snake is retransformed into a magical snake that can finally put out the fire.

That the children are able to collaborate on the interwoven realistic-fantasy themes depends on some common understanding about vacations, about the house and its layout, and about the mutual responsibilities of Husband and Wife. The collaboration also depends on mastery of social play conventions. Both children are able to omit and accept the other's omission of many details in what might be a realistic enactment of taking a vacation (packing, traveling, checking into and out of the hotel). Each is able to pick up on sudden shifts in theme—such as from that of vacation to that of monster, and from normal domestic life to what becomes a conflagration—and to join the other in repetition of components that seem interesting (giving over the earnings, putting out the fire). Success in playing the shifting scenario rests on the continuous verbal communication of plans and on the description or identification of essential pretend states of affairs, as well as of object transformations and inventions.

Mature role play can use the resources of roles and themes in either of two ways: The roles may be adopted and the plot or themes acted out, or dolls can be used as the characters and made to go through the action, which is usually simultaneously narrated. Both techniques are based on the same knowledge of roles and social events, and both may display the features of repetitiveness, stereotyping, schematization, and realism-fantasy mixture. Adopting the roles and acting out was used exclusively by the children in our sample, perhaps because few dolls and no setting replicas (dollhouses or fire station) were provided. The other technique was observed by Nelson and Gruendel (1979). Provision of replicas, often with modeling or prompting by an adult, has been used to elicit role knowledge (Watson and Fisher, 1980) and to study the expressive content of play (Erikson, 1951). The existence of the two techniques points again to the abstract nature of the information that permits social phenomena and pretend procedures to be represented in different forms. One important difference between the two techniques is that a crucial aspect of spontaneous pretend play is reduced or altogether absent unless two or more children are interactionally engaged in the play with replicas and thus have *at the same time* the tasks of depicting the pretend scenario and managing the social interaction of the two or more actual partners. In social role play, the children are simultaneously interacting both as age-mates (and perhaps also as friends) and as the role personas they have adopted.

Enactment Techniques in Children's Role Play

Enactment techniques in mature role play include both verbal and nonverbal means of representing an adopted role and the relevant action sequence. There have been few studies of the means by which children represent a character's behavior nonverbally. Considerable detail can be portrayed in certain phases of the action—for example, Mother may pretend to button up Baby's dress, fluff out the skirt, and examine the effect, but other phases may be only fleetingly indicated or even omitted. Expressive gestures, which we can identify only impressionistically and react to as we might to properly contexted adult displays, are often highly skilled and stereotyped renditions. For example, an older girl expressed bitter grief as she bent over a dead pet. She wailed to her Mother, "Mommy, mommy, my pet, he's dead!" She wept over the body (a large teddy bear), bent her shoulders and head, rocked back and forth rhythmically, and sobbed.

The first basic means for role representation are selection, performance of action, and indication of attitude appropriate to the persona of the role relationship. Not only is the Child relatively helpless, demanding, and sometimes naughty, and the Mother capable and nurturant, although sometimes exasperated, but each also expects the other to take the complementary stance and perform the complementary actions (Garvey, 1979a). A second means for role representation is the use of in-role speech. In-role speech uses the appropriate register for the character in the depicted role relationship and setting. Mother speaks with Father or with a neighbor Mother quite differently from the way she speaks with her own Child. Children's ability to produce such differentiated speech has been studied by sociolinguists as evidence that children know the social structuring that underlies the distribution of speech variants and their co-occurrence in social registers. Children's command of "Motherese" in role play has been investigated by Sachs and Devin (1976), while speech in the nuclear family, in a school setting, and in a doctor's office has been studied by Andersen (1977). Three findings are of particular interest here.

First, while verisimilitude in speech register during role play generally improves with age and with the child's experience of different social events and types of persons, representation relies heavily on certain features that are presumably salient to young children, and which for older children may have become stylized manners of indicating a role. For example, pretend Mothers raise the pitch of their voices and widen the pitch excursion when speaking to Babies. Fathers' voices are lower pitched and gruffer.

Second, role relationships are differentiated. For example, the situation of a Father speaking with a doctor can be indicated by further lowering of the doctor's voice to suggest the higher status of the doctor in his office relative to the Father of a Child patient.

Third, virtually all levels of language and speech organization can be used for the representation of a role, although prosodic and paralinguistic features, the lexicon, and pragmatic features are invoked more frequently and more accurately than are variants from the phonological, morphological, and syntactic levels. In particular, the pragmatic aspects of speech, including the selection and placement of speech acts and the variant formulations that reflect dimensions of politeness and other interpersonal orientations, are represented in the earliest stages of role play. Mother is likely to ask the Child, "Would you like some milk?" but the Child is likely to say, "I want my milk." The consensus of the research conducted until now suggests that roles are portrayed by the use of speech-register features, but that these are not consistently deployed, and that, furthermore, many co-occurrence rules of the registers are not observed.

Production and Regulation Techniques in Children's Role Play

Production and regulation techniques include a number of different message functions. The most important one is that of making the pretend transformation—changing the playroom into a doctor's office, or changing oneself or a playmate into Mother. If their intended prelocutionary effect is achieved (that is, if the partner assents to the transformation), such messages not only set the players into the pretend framework but also change the setting, the object, or the individual into the new persona. The formula "I'll be the mommy and you be the baby," if accepted, brings that state of affairs into being. Within an ongoing pretend activity, saying, "This is the train" while pointing to the sofa both sustains the pretend framework and brings about the change in the object for the purposes of play. Indirect expressions are also effective; for example, "Drink your soup" produces soup in an empty bowl. Role transformations, too, may be implicit. It is a convention of play, already familiar to three-year-olds, that explicit assignment of one relational role implies that the partner has adopted the role complement. If a child says, "Won't you be my baby, Baby?" and if the partner nods, the speaker has also transformed herself into the Mother of that Baby.

Several conventions appear to operate in the regulation of children's role play. One convention in role play is virtually inviolable. It might read: If one person adopts a role, the partner must also adopt a role if he is to join the play. This will be called the "I be/you be" rule; it is not possible to play Batman or Mother to the real partner's everyday identity. Another convention is that the roles must be selected from the same realm, thus permitting joint action in the same pretend setting. For example, if one child adopts the role of Superman, the partner may join if she accepts the proferred role of Wonderwoman. If she refuses, she may watch as Superman drives off to join Robin, but otherwise she can only pretend alone in a different realm—for example, becoming Mother to a Baby (doll). The two partners may then communicate about what each is doing, each in his separate realm. For example, the girl may inform the boy, "I'm putting Baby to bed," but the two children do not act within the other's pretend world. This convention will be called the rule of compatible roles. During a play session, roles may be exchanged or new scenarios may entail the adoption of quite different roles. In either case, the role assignments are renegotiated; in the case of a new scenario, objects and settings must also be changed.

In addition to messages that bring about the pretend transformations, there are also communications devoted to adjusting or improving the production of joint play. A child occupying the role of Baby may briefly "break frame" and correct her partner's rendition of Father, as did a three-year-old girl who found Father was not stern enough to her persona of naughty Baby. She modeled for the partner the manner in which he should shout at Baby. When he got it right, she resumed her petulant Baby voice and, with it, the Baby role.

The course of role play does not run smoothly, and most episodes include some frame breaks, in which the role partners change back to their normal identities, using their own voices and gestures to discuss or argue about something in the role-play frame or else some event in the actual environment (for example, a child may ask in response to a sound outside the playroom, "What's that noise?") Children may also break frame to discuss a memory or a plan from real life (for example, "When my mommy comes, we're going to get ice cream.") After age three, comments and discussions concerning the play framework become common: One child rejected a plan to meet a monster, saying, "I don't want to play that. It's too scary." As another child was gobbling up pretend cookies and offering them to his partner, the latter said, "I don't see any cookies. You were just pretending." From the age of three onward, children often question acts of their partners that they cannot interpret unambiguously, asking whether the act was "for real" or "just pretend."

Other regulation techniques in role play include invitations to play and discussions of what to play ("Let's play"; "What do you want to play?"; "Let's play fireman"). The frequent pairing of the words "just" or "only" with "pretend," the ubiquity of discussion about enactment procedures, and the explicit comments devoted to arranging the joint imaginary experience (called "connection and disconnection" statements by Schwartzman, 1978) all suggest that children are aware of the play framework as a special and distinct experience. Termination of the episode is often explicit: "I'm tired. I don't want to play anymore." On occasion, a just-completed episode may be evaluated; "That was fun," for example, said at the end of a successful dragon-slaying bout. By three years of age, pretending is viewed by most children as distinct from the paramount reality of everyday life. Perhaps the most dramatic behavioral contrast between role-play and nonplay orientations is the switch from in-role to nonrole speech. A detectable change occurs when, for example, a Mother interrupts her crooning monologue to Baby (a doll) and informs a partner, "In a minute they will bring us some orange juice and cookies."

The production and regulation techniques we observe in our sample suggest that conventional procedures for playing together have been acquired by young children. Objectification of knowledge about role playing is evidenced by the fact that "errors" in procedures and in role content are often corrected by a partner. These corrections indicate an ability to detect and repair features of the production that are incompatible with a role or a theme. Furthermore, jokes can be made about the basic rule of sex-appropriate role adoption. Joking is rather more dangerous than error correction, in that a partner might take offense at, say, an intentional misassignment of a female role to a male partner (and, thus, the act might be construed as teasing or insulting). Blatant misassignments, however, can be made and taken as humorous. Joking and correction of errors indicate metacognitive operations on an underlying rule-based system of play procedures.

Thus, for the achievement of social role play, it is not sufficient for players to have attained the level of cognitive development that permits revocable transformation of self and other (doll or partner). Players must also be able to collaborate with willing and capable partners in executing the play. The communicative conventions that produce and sustain the play and make this collaboration possible must be acquired before role play can occur. Players must hear and correctly interpret the shifts in speech style, gestures, and content of talk that guide the interaction in and across the realms of pretend and nonpretend.

The Development of Social Role Play

Two trajectories may be traced in the development of social role play. One involves the adoption and assignment of roles and the other concerns the incorporation of a partner into pretend action. The first trajectory follows one individual's transition from functional-role enactment through relational-role enactment to relational-role adoption. The other trajectory represents movement from explicit communication about functional-role activity and participation in such activity through discussion of others' role enactments to eventual active participation in joint relational-role play.

Attainment along these two trajectories was clearly exhibited by the majority of the dyads in our youngest group (2:10-3:3), although several did not develop extended plots after assuming roles. Analyses of their most skilled and extended performances have been provided elsewhere (Garvey, 1979a; 1979b). The leading role-players among these dyads were girls. Preferred roles were those of the nuclear family, and the favorite themes were domestic.

A new longitudinal collection of the dyadic interactions of two-year-olds with their best friends and with their mothers has captured several of the precursory steps toward the achievement of social role play. Three middle-class children have been videotaped at monthly intervals for five months. They were observed in the laboratory playroom, each child alone with the best friend, at home with the friend, at home with the mother doing familiar tasks, and in play situations selected by each mother–child pair. Taping sessions varied from thirty minutes to one hour. Mothers also made biweekly audio recordings of their normal activities with their children. Age at the onset of the study and sex of the target child and the friend are as follows: Dyad 1 — Sarah (2:2) and Becky (2:10); Dyad 2 — Judy (2:4) and Tom (2:5); Dyad 3 — Jack (2:6) and Anne (2:7). Dyads 2 and 3 were at similar stages in pretend development and changed in the same way over the observation period. For brevity, therefore only Dyad 2's episodes will be quoted. In Dyad 1, Sarah and Becky were unevenly matched in age and in pretend development: Sarah was still struggling with the basic requirement of flexible shifting to the pretend framework. The problems she had engaging in pretend play with Becky and with her own mother are highly instructive, however, and will also be cited.

Figure 1 summarizes the changes in the individual child's play behavior (left-hand column) between the ages of two and three and indicates the parallel behavior of a peer partner (right-hand column). At the same time, peer involvement may be understood to indicate the uses a child can make of a peer partner. The center column indicates some of the requirements for the achieved level of peer participation. It should be noted that the progression of phases does not imply sequential replacement of prior phases; functional-role enactment may be observed either in solitary or collaborative form, even among older dyads. Relational-role enactment and play require a role counterpart, but this function may be served, even for older children, by a doll or an imagined person. The sequential arrangement of the phases results from the fact that relational-role enactment with a doll and relational-role play with a doll and then with a peer were added, without exception in our samples, in chrono-

Figure 1. Changes During the Third Year of Life in the Use of Social Roles and of a Peer Partner

	Characterization of Play	Requirements	Activity of the Partner
Phase 1	Functional-role enactment: Child sets table, drives car somewhere, speaks on telephone.	Recognize other's pretend orientation; have some knowledge of specific "script"; verbalize any transformation.	Partner performs same enactment in imitation or briefly joins in complementary functional role.
Phase 2	Relational-role enactment: Child portrays a role relative to a role complement (Mother to Baby [doll]), without claiming to be that persona.	Recognize the specific role relationship being enacted; discriminate between speech used for enactment and about enactment.	Partner attends to the performance as audience, but participates by talking about the pretend roles and action. May also engage in a different pretend activity.

In the transition from Phase 2 to Phase 3, a pretending child may claim a transformed role identity, but does not go on to act in that role. The child partner attempts and is sometimes permitted to perform some act consonant with the "script" (fetching the bottle for Mother to give to Baby [doll]), but neither claims nor is assigned a relational role.

| Phase 3 | Relational-role adoption: Child claims a relational role and acts consistently in that role; child assigns partner a complementary or compatible role. | Understand role-assignment techniques; be able and willing to accept identity transformation; either generate or accept instruction for appropriate role performance. | Partner acts in an assigned or adopted role within same "script." |

logical order. In the earliest sessions recorded, functional-role enactment was observed both in solitary and social form.

In Phase 1, both children engage in functional-role play. Although each child may be occupied with a different theme (for example, one enacts a telephone call while the other "drives" the car on some errand), both children may also take turns enacting the same theme (for example, one watches, awaits a turn, and then drives the car when the other has finished). There may also be loose coordination between themes (for example, both begin a pretend meal, but then one drives off to get some sugar and doesn't come back, while the partner continues with the meal). Given the fact that almost all the pretend activity is verbalized (see also Ungerer and others, 1981) each partner can keep informed of the other's plan and thus can join in at any time. The communications, however, are usually more interactionally purposeful; each questions the other concerning the pretend activity, and even when "just watching," one partner is likely to make suggestions about the other's play.

Example 1. *Judy (2:4) and Tom (2:5) share a brief functional-role enactment, as Judy prepares coffee and serves it to Tom.*

J. Here's your coffee. (Hands cup.)	T. (Drinks.) Mmm, that was good. That was good, Judy.
J. Good. Good, here's a plate. This broken-one plate. In here. (Takes plate from box.)	T. Here, there....
J. Want sugar? (Offers bowl.)	T. Sugar. (Takes bowl.)
J. Sugar?	T. Okay
J. Milk? Sugar, no. Sugar? (Ends by whispering to herself.)	(Turns to toy trucks, losing interest in meal.)

In Phase 2, one child engages in relational-role enactment. In a mixed-sex dyad, this is always the girl, and the roles are those of Caregiver and Baby (a doll). Two girls together care for the doll or dolls. In Phase 2, the child enacting mothering behavior does not explicitly adopt the role of Mother. In the following typical segment, the girl's plans are elicited by the boy's questioning.

Example 2. *Judy (2:4) holds and hugs the doll, following a long monologue in "motherese" to the doll. Tom (2:5) watches and then approaches her and reaches toward the doll.*

J. I'm gonna take my baby and then I'm gonna... (to Tom) Don't touch it because I'm gonna... (Hugs and makes sympathy noise to doll.) Oooh.	T. Is that a baby?
J. No, don't touch, 'cause the baby's tired.	T. Is the baby tired?
J. No, the baby's not tired. Gonna put her to bed. Gonna rest her.	

J. I'm gonna take the baby for a walk. First I'm gonna take the baby to the park and then I'm take the baby at the... park.

T. What's the baby gonna.... What's Judy gonna do with the baby?

T. And then you gonna come back home with the baby?

J. Yeah, please, 'cause I'm going now into the store and then wave goodbye to you and going to take her home now and then have to go out to the store first.

While still in Phase 2, the child enacting Mother also directs the Baby (doll) to speak, sometimes speaks for the Baby (raising voice pitch still higher), and maintains while in play a flow of "motherese" monologue, interspersed with comments to the partner about the pretend activity. Speech to the partner, speech to the doll, and speech for the doll are differentiated.

Example 3. *Judy (2:5) carries and croons to the doll as Tom (2:7) watches. She gets on the toy car with the doll.*

T. Is that the baby?

J. Yeah. *(To doll)* All right? Baby. Sit right... *(To Tom)* She's gonna sit right here. *(To doll)* You want your momma? All right, let me get your momma. *(Fetches larger doll.)* The babysitter's coming today. The baby and the momma. *(To doll)* See momma. Talk to ma. Talk to ma. Go talk, say, "Ge" *(Speaks as Baby speaking to larger doll.)* Momma. Mommy.

J. Mmhum.

T. Is that the baby?
T. Where's the mommy?

J Right... I got her lap. *(Shows him larger doll.)* I got her all ready. *(As she prepares to drive off, Tom shows her how to shift the gears on the car.)*

During Phase 2 boys indicate their interest in mothering play and some knowledge of mothering procedures and infant habits by questions and comments about "the baby" or "the dolly." In the later sessions, both Tom and Jack succeeded in offering something to the Baby their girl partners were mothering, although neither boy adopted or was assigned a role title. In the next example, an attempt at parallel-role enactment was flawed by a category error (a little car cannot serve as Baby). The boy's move was not fully intelligible to the girl. This particular segment followed the boy's attempt to touch the Baby (doll) in its cradle, an attempt the girl vigorously protested.

Example 4. *Judy (2:6) has just forbidden Tom (2:7) to touch the cradle. She moves his hand off the cradle and sings "Rock-A-Bye, Baby" to the doll.*

J. She's sleeping.

T. *(Comes near cradle with a little car.)* I have a baby, too. I have a baby car to sleep, too. I have a baby car to sleep, too. *(Moves to put car in cradle.)*

J. A baby car to sleep, too? *Picks up the doll as he approaches.)* Don't, Tom, 'cause the baby's sleeping.

T. Well, can I put the baby car to sleep?

J. All right. It's just for a little bit of time. It can go here. *(Points to place in cradle.)*

Talk during Phase 2 indicates that, for both partners, the concept of nuclear-family roles is well developed; it is as if the roles are ready and waiting to be filled by the right individual. In this phase, however, even the child enacting the role of Mother to Baby (a doll) makes comments that indicate she has not actually identified herself as Mother in any explicit way. Baby's Mother is often elsewhere (for example, at the library or at home). The following example illustrates the near approach to role adoption during this transition period.

Example 5. *Judy (2:7) has just hugged the Baby (a doll) and made sympathy noises to it. Tom (2:8) watches. His first question seems to be in response to the sympathy noise.*

T. What's the matter with baby?

J. She's crying.

T. Why's she crying?

J. Well, she wants her mom, actually.

T. Is Raggedy Ann the mama?

J. Um, she's at home. Well, she's not the mama. *(Looks*

	at Raggedy Ann.) She's just... well, she just fun.
	T. Where's the dada?
J. Oh.	
	T. Is the dada at work?
J. The dada's at work. Um, well, someday you can see the dada.	

After a brief diversion, Judy announces to Tom in a loud voice, "I'm the mommy." This statement was the first explicit role claim she had made. It represents the transition to Phase 3 of relational-role adoption. Concomitant involvement of the partner in a reciprocal role did not, however, occur for this dyad.

Phase 3, defined as mutual and reciprocal relational-role play, was not achieved over the five monthly sessions for Dyads 2 and 3. We subsequently paired the two girls from these dyads, when Judy was 2:10 and Anne was 3:1. As a dyad, they adopted the roles of Mothers to two Babies (dolls) and took the Babies off to the park together. While both occupied the relational roles with respect to the dolls, they intereacted with each other as two Mothers, sharing their concern about the Babies. The two girls also played at doctor and patient (reciprocal occupational roles), and they took turns in each role, each using the other as role counterpart. In general, then, their play at this age represents the achievement of Phase 3 and is comparable to the role play observed in the dyads of the age group (2:10–3:3) previously observed.

The ability to join a peer partner in pretend play depends on the ability not only to recognize the other's pretend orientation, but also to recognize the particular plan or theme proposed and follow the transformations the partner makes. The shared functional-role enactments of Dyads 2 and 3, even in their earliest sessions together, indicated that these abilities were present. In Dyad 1, Sarah (2:2), the youngest child in this sample, was also able to join her older friend, Becky (2:8), in joint pretend tea parties and in alternating bouts of driving the car somewhere or telephoning (all functional-role enactments). Not all Becky's transformations, however, were comprehended by Sarah. In the following example, Sarah appears to understand that Becky is driving somewhere in the car, but she fails to follow the next implied transformation.

Example 6. *Sarah (2:4) watches Becky (3:0) as the latter steers the car.*

	B. Beep! Beep!
S. Where you going?	
	B. Get out of the way. Get out of the road, all right?
S. What road?	
	B. The one I'm driving in. There's a lot of traffic in here. I'm driving in my car.

S. No, this is a rug. *(Looking down at the rug.)*

B. No, it isn't. It's a road. Wanna feel it?

Sarah's play with her mother and with Becky clearly demonstrates both the importance of learning the language of role play and the strong probability that conventions of role-play communication are acquired prior to gaining the ability to perform the pretend transformation of oneself to another's role persona. In sessions with her mother, Sarah had ample opportunity to learn how to communicate transformation of objects, settings, and persons. Sarah's mother encouraged her to "be the mommy" to her dolls and also proposed playing Baby to Sarah's role of Mommy. Sarah, however, was unable or unwilling to accept this transformation, although under her mother's direction she did enact mothering behavior to dolls.

Example 6. *With her mother's active encouragement, Sarah (2:3) has put her dolls to sleep and sung to them. Sarah then brings a book to her mother.*

S. Pick book for you to read.

M. Well, aren't you gonna read that to the baby doll? You're the mommy.

S. But you're the mommy. I'm not the mommy.

M. What're you?

S. I'm the Sarah.

The verbal convention of role transformation was probably learned from sessions with her mother. In sessions with her peer, Sarah began to use the basic role-transformation formula, but her behavior indicated that she had not grasped its full significance. In her second peer session, when she was 2:4 and Becky was 3:0, she followed Becky's instructions for sitting on a chair, putting her feet up, and looking up at the light—enacting the role of patient to Becky's dentist, although the action involved was "drying and combing hair." After they exchanged positions and Becky sat in the chair, Sarah proposed, "You be the dentist and I be that one, and I be gonna...okay?"; but she performs no further role-consonant action. In the following session (Example 7), Sarah showed that she had grasped the "I be/you be" rule, but again she failed to perform role-consonant behavior and, we assume, had failed to make the role transformation of herself.

Example 7. *Becky (3:1) has adopted the role of Mother to the Baby (a doll) and has taken it to Sunday school. Sarah (2:5) has been watching and talking with Becky about the play, although performing no role enactment herself. Becky lays the doll on the couch.*

B. She can lie right here for the dentist to get her, all right?

S. I'm the dentist!

S. And what can you be?

S. I'm gonna... I wanna drive that baby to Sunday school.

B. I know you are. She can be the patient.

B. I'm gonna be the mother driving her to you, all right?

B. Well, I'm gonna drive this baby to the dentist, all right? And you can drive this baby to Sunday school after I bring the car back, all right?

Although she was armed with the pretending formula, reciprocal role enactment for the unfamiliar roles and typical action line of dentist and patient was still not possible for Sarah, and she has not as yet shown that she is ready to adopt any relational role with her friend. It is difficult to see how she might come to collaborate in such play without constant communication with her partner concerning the pretend activity, since such activity is formed and conducted primarily on the verbal level.

A longitudinal collection of home video recordings of three younger females with their mothers (Miller, 1982) provides observations of a yet earlier stage (beginning for the three girls at 1:3, 2:0, and 2:1, respectively) and of a lower socioeconomic-level group. Miller's video records and the recordings of our own subjects Judy, Jack, and Sarah at home with their mothers indicate strong parental support for and active participation in the enactment and production techniques of pretend play. In addition, the girls also received explicit and often very detailed modeling and instruction in mothering play with dolls. The mothers modeled the "motherese" appropriate to infants, which differed from their normal speech to the three girls themselves. They demonstrated (or instructed the children to perform) affectional, nurturant, instructional, and disciplinary behaviors toward the Baby (a doll) — all categories of behavior that Judy and Anne also directed to dolls in their relational-role enactments in the peer sessions (Miller and Garvey, 1981). For any given episode, the child was more likely than the mother was to initiate the mothering play. Once it was begun, however (by the child picking up a doll, for example), the mothers promptly began to interpret, extend, and elaborate the play by proposing plans and attributing appropriate acts, states, or needs to the Baby (a doll) and by reminding the child of the Mother–Baby relationship: "She's hungry. You have to heat her bottle."

Conclusion

The preceding account of social role play development adds the dimensions of interpersonal communication and conventionalization of pretend procedures to the individual cognitive changes believed to enable the growth of such play. The abilities to conceptualize self–other relations, perform revocable transformations of objects and settings, and recognize or plan coherent action lines as plots or scripts set upper limits to the pretend play behavior a young child exhibits. Other factors also operate, however, in the acquisition and elaboration of role play. Parental support of the girls' mothering play with dolls, for example, may well have been a factor in accounting for the girls' more advanced skill and greater enthusiasm for enactments of mothering, as compared with the boys in our samples (see also McLoyd, 1980).

The starting point for the growth of social role play is the child's spontaneous experimentation with the conventional uses of objects and replicas. Most caregivers respond to children's imitative acts by acknowledging their intelligibility and by elaborating the children's intentions. Caregivers also model and often explicitly instruct children in the conventions of pretending. Children's tendency to verbalize their own actions and immediate plans happens to mesh, conveniently, with the requirement that pretend transformations and attributions be made clear to one's partner. Children first learn to share functional-role enactments with their caregivers; in the process, they learn many of the techniques for marking the pretend state and for indicating specific transformations — smacking one's lips to indicate pleasure at the taste of imaginary tea, warning one's partner that the play stove is "hot," or making engine sounds while moving a toy truck.

Dolls, toy animals, or puppets permit or actually seem to invite the reproduction of familiar actions and the attribution of needs, attitudes, and intentions to a person-substitute. Mothers collaborate with their children in verbally formulating these attributions and their usual consequents, thereby producing little scripts: "Baby's tired? Why don't you put her to bed? Now, cover her up and sing her a song." Pretend "motherese," which constitutes the primary enactment technique in mothering play, is also demonstrated. Thus, children do have an opportunity to learn and practice role-enactment procedures in a supportive interpersonal environment where discussion about the play alternates with role-appropriate talk and action. Comments by children in our samples, as well as several unsuccessful attempts by their mothers to encourage explicit role adoption (similar to the attempt cited in Example 6), suggest that children may pass through a phase of relatively advanced role-enactment ability (a phase that would include learning the formula for role adoption and assignment) before they come to realize that they are indeed being a Mommy to a doll or to their own mothers' enactments of Baby.

Sharing functional-role enactment with a peer partner in the middle of the third year of life is possible, even probable, for friends who have some expertise in pretending procedures. If, for reasons of sex or immaturity, a partner is unable to collaborate in relational-role enactment, then young girls will enact the roles of Mother and Baby, using a doll as Baby (but will never use the doll as Mother to self as Baby). The relatively unskilled partner, however, need only recognize the pretend orientation to engage the pretending child in discussion about the role enactment. Thus, the function of the partner is similar to that of the child's mother—providing interested attention, making suggestions for further action, and responding to the pretending child's inventions. Although the partner's motives and level of skill differ from those of the mother, the partner shares with the mother the need to interpret the pretend behavior as meaningful and to understand the pretending child's actions and plans for action. (From a practical point of view, the partner must distinguish between speech addressed to him and speech addressed to the pretend Baby.)

The process of communicating about the role enactments, as well as the need to identify publicly not only the relevant object and action transformations but also the persons occupying the positions in the basic relational-role schema, contribute to eventual role adoption. At that point, assignment of a role position complementary to the partner's is necessary if the play is to be shared. The partner comes to be seen as a potential candidate for the position of role complement and will be assigned, as appropriate, the role of Father, Baby, or Big Sister. Judy might correctly have predicted to Tom at the end of Example 5: "Some day you can *be* the dada," for in only a few months she would probably have attempted to assign him the role of Father.

References

Andersen, E. A. "Learning to Speak with Style: A Study of the Sociolinguistic Skills of Children." Unpublished doctoral dissertation, Stanford University, 1977.

Erikson, E. "Sex Differences in Play Configurations of Pre-Adolescents." *American Journal of Orthopsychiatry,* 1951, *21* (4), 667–692.

Fein, G. "Pretend Play in Childhood: An Integrative Review." *Child Development,* 1981, *52* (4), 1095–1118.

Garvey, C. "An Approach to the Study of Children's Role Play." *The Quarterly Newsletter of the Laboratory of Comparative Human Cognition,* 1979a, *1* (4), 69–73.

Garvey, C. "Communicational Controls in Social Play." In B. Sutton-Smith (Ed.), *Play and Learning.* New York: Gardner Press, 1979b.

Garvey, C., and Berndt, R., "The Organization of Pretend Play." *Catalog of Selected Documents in Psychology,* 1977, *7,* Ms. no. 1589.

Huttenlocher, J., and Higgins, E. T. "Issues in the Study of Symbolic Development." In W. A. Collins (Ed.), *Minnesota Symposium on Child Psychology.* Vol. 11. Minneapolis: University of Minnesota Press, 1978.

Kavanaugh, R., Whittington, S., and Cerbone, M. "Mothers' Use of Fantasy in Speech to Young Children." Paper presented at the Biennial Convention of the Society for Research in Child Development, Boston, April 2–5, 1981.

Lieberman, A. F. "Preschoolers' Competence with a Peer: Relations with Attachment and Peer Experience." *Child Development,* 1977, *48* (4), 1277–1287.

McLoyd, V. "Verbally Expressed Modes of Transformation in the Fantasy Play of Black Preschool Children." *Child Development,* 1980, *51* (4), 1133–1139.

Miller, P. S. *Amy, Wendy, and Beth: Learning Language in South Baltimore.* Austin: University of Texas Press, 1982.

Miller, P. S., and Garvey, C. "Learning to Mother at Two." Paper presented at the Biennial Convention of the Society for Research in Child Development, Boston, April 2–5, 1981.

Nelson, K., and Gruendel, J. M. "At Morning It's Lunchtime: A Scriptal View of Children's Dialogues." *Discourse Processes,* 1979, *2* (2), 73-94.

Sachs, J. "The Role of Adult-Child Play in Language Development." In K. Rubin (Ed.), *Children's Play.* San Francisco: Jossey-Bass, in press.

Sachs, J., and Devin, J. "Young Children's Use of Age-Appropriate Speech Styles in Social Interaction and Role Playing." *Journal of Child Language,* 1976, *3* (1), 81-98.

Schwartzman, H. *Transformations: The Anthropology of Children's Play.* New York: Plenum, 1978.

Ungerer, J., Zelazo, P., Kearsley, R., and O'Leary, K. "Developmental Changes in the Representation of Objects in Symbolic Play from 18 to 34 Months of Age." *Child Development,* 1981, *52* (1), 186-195.

Winner, E., McCarthy, M., Kleinman, S., and Gardner, H. "First Metaphors." In H. Gardner and D. Wolf (Eds.), *New Directions for Child Development: Early Symbolization,* no. 3. San Francisco: Jossey-Bass, 1979.

Catherine Garvey is professor and senior research scientist at the Department of Psychology of The Johns Hopkins University in Baltimore, Maryland.

Index

A

Abelson, R. P., 10, 26
Ackerman, B. P., 37, 41, 44
Ainsworth, M. D. S., 49, 50, 51, 52, 59
Andersen, E. A., 88, 100
Anzai, Y., 7, 25
Asher, S. R., 30, 33, 34, 38, 44
Attachment, mother-child: Analysis of research on, 47-60; background on, 47-51; discussion of, 57-59; goal-corrected phase of, 49, 50, 54, 56, 57, 58; methods of analyzing, 53-55; and preseparation behavior, 53; research method for, 51-55; results of study of, 55-57; and reunion behavior, 53-54; and separation questions, 52, 54-55, 56-57; and strange situation, 51-53
Atwood, M. E., 25
August, D. L., 44
Austin, J. L., 37, 44

B

Baillargeon, R., 10, 25
Bakeman, R., 63, 77
Baker, L., 6, 25
Baldwin, J., 1, 3
Bank Street College of Education, research at, 5, 15
Bates, E., 62, 77
Bates, K. R., 38, 39, 42, 45
Beal, C. R., 37, 44
Bearison, D. J., 39, 44
Belle, D., 64-65, 77
Bergman, A., 48, 60
Berndt, R., 84, 100
Blehar, M. C., 47, 59
Blurton Jones, N., 47, 59
Botkin, P. T., 44
Bowlby, J., 48-49, 55, 59, 64, 77
Bromley, D. B., 49, 59
Brown, A. L., 6, 14, 23, 25, 29, 44
Brownlee, J., 63, 77
Bruce, B., 7, 25
Bruner, J. S., 1, 3, 42, 44
Budwig, N. A., 26

Bullock, M., 10, 25
Burke, K., 9, 25
Byrne, R., 12, 25

C

Cambridge Public School System, 67
Campbell, E., 78
Carter, D. B., 45
Case, R., 9, 25
Cerbone, M., 84, 100
Chi, M. T. H., 18, 25
Children: at six to eight months, 48; at one year, 49; at two years, 48-49, 50, 82, 83, 91-98; at three years, 48-49, 50, 51-58, 89-90; at four years, 32, 33, 34-35, 36, 38, 39-40, 50, 51-58, 82, 85; at five years, 32, 33, 34-35, 36, 37, 38, 39-40, 66-77; at six years, 32, 33, 34-35, 37, 38, 39, 40; at seven years, 37, 38, 66-77; at eight years, 15-23, 37, 39; at nine years, 15-23, 33, 38; at ten years, 39; at eleven years, 15-23; at twelve years, 15-23; at thirteen years, 38; at fourteen years, 38
Cirillo, L., 5n, 6, 26
Cohen, L. J., 48, 59
Cole, M., 35, 45
Communication: background on, 29-31; components of skills in referential, 31-41; development of skills in, 29-46; further research for, 41-44; listener skills in, 36-39; and perspective taking, 32, 34-35; and social role play, 81-101; speaker skills in, 32-36
Corsaro, W., 65, 68, 75, 78
Corsini, D. A., 47, 60
Cosgrove, J. M., 30, 36, 39, 42, 44, 45

D

Danner, F. W., 36, 42, 45
Decontextualization, in social role play, 82
DeLoache, J. S., 14, 23, 25, 29, 44
Development, concept of, 5

103

Devin, J., 88, 101
Dewey, J., 7, 25
Dittman, A. T., 39, 44
Docherty, E. M., 57, 60
Dodge, K. A., 62, 78
Dore, J., 63, 78
Dowley McNamee, G., 26
Draguns, J., 24, 25

E

Edwards, C., 76, 78
Ericcson, K. A., 14, 20, 25
Erikson, E., 87, 100
Ernst, G. W., 10, 25

F

Fein, G., 82, 100
Feldman, S. S., 47, 48, 59, 60
Feltovich, P. J., 18, 25
Fikes, R. E., 10, 25
Flavell, J. H., 8, 23, 24, 25, 26, 29–30, 33, 36, 37, 38, 39, 42, 44–45, 46, 55, 60
Fondacaro, R., 31, 45
Forbes, D., 1–4, 5n, 61–79
Fry, C. L., 44

G

Galanter, E., 1, 4, 7, 26, 30, 45, 59, 60, 78
Gardner, H., 101
Garvey, C., 2, 3, 62–63, 68, 78, 81–101
Gearhart, M., 23, 25
Gelman, R., 10, 25
Glaser, R., 18, 25
Glucksberg, S., 30, 31, 32, 33, 34, 36, 45
Goal state: defining, 7–9; redefining, 11
Goals: and economy of action, 8–9; feasibility of, 7–8; flexibility of, 9; setting of, in planning, 15–16, 41; value maximization for, 9
Goldin, S. E., 10, 11, 12, 13, 25
Gonso, J., 30, 45
Gottman, J., 30, 45, 63, 65, 66, 68, 78
Grant Foundation, William T., 47n
Green, F. L., 44
Greenberg, M. T., 1–4, 32, 45, 47–60
Gruendel, J. M., 14, 26, 62, 78, 87, 101

H

Haslett, B., 62–63, 78
Hayes-Roth, B., 10, 11, 12, 13, 25
Hayes-Roth, F., 12, 13, 25
Higgins, E. T., 30, 31, 32, 33, 34, 36, 45, 83, 100
Huttenlocher, J., 83, 100
Huvelle, N., 68, 78

I

Ingham, M. E., 47, 59
Inhelder, B., 59, 60
Ironsmith, M., 36, 45

J

Jacklin, C., 66, 76, 78
Jeffries, R., 12, 25
Jewson, J., 5n, 15, 20, 26

K

Kaplan, B., 5, 25, 63, 78
Karabenick, J. D., 36, 39, 45
Katz, M. M., 2, 61–79
Kavanaugh, R., 84, 100
Kearsley, R., 101
Kendall, P. C., 24, 26, 42, 43, 46
Kessel, F. S., 55, 60
Kister, M. C., 30, 36, 38, 39, 45
Klahr, D., 23, 25, 62, 78
Kleinman, S., 101
Kotarbinski, T., 7, 8, 9, 26
Kotsonis, M. E., 45
Krauss, R. M., 30, 31, 32, 33, 34, 36, 45
Kreutzer, M. A., 8, 26
Kushner, S., 8, 26

L

Lakoff, R., 63, 78
Keach, G., 47, 59
Leonard, C., 8, 26
Leont'ev, A. M., 23, 26
Levey, L. M., 39, 44
Levy, F. K., 9, 26
Lewis, M., 48, 60
Lieberman, A. F., 47, 59, 84, 100
Listeners: components of skills of, 36–39; and message adequacy, 37–39; and responses to messages, 39; role knowledge by, 36–37

Livesley, W. G., 49, 59
Lorenz, K., 81
Lubin, D., 2, 61-79

M

McCann, D. C., 31, 45
McCarthy, M., 101
Maccoby, E., 47, 48, 49, 59-60, 66, 76, 78
McGrew, W. C., 65, 78
McLane, J. B., 26
McLoyd, V., 99, 100
Mahler, M. S., 48, 60
Mallay, H., 64-65, 78
Markman, E. M., 39, 45
Marvin, R. S., 2, 32, 45, 47-60
Massad, C. M., 39, 45
Meacham, J. A., 8, 26
Mead, G. H., 64, 78
Metaplanning, principles of, 7
Miller, G. A., 1, 4, 7, 26, 30, 45, 59, 60, 78
Miller, P. H., 55, 60
Miller P. S., 98, 100
Miller, S. A., 36, 39, 45
Moscowitz, D. S., 47, 60
Mossler, D. G., 32, 45, 57, 59, 60
Mother-child attachment. *See* Attachment, mother-child
Murphy, J., 78

N

National Institute of Mental Health, 61n
National Science Foundation, 61n
Nelson, K., 14, 26, 62, 78, 87, 101
Newell, A., 9, 10, 25, 26
Newman, D., 5n, 7, 23, 25
Nilsson, N. J., 10, 25

O

Object substitution, in social role play, 82
O'Brien, C., 45
O'Brien, R. G., 45
Oden, S. L., 33, 44
O'Leary, K., 101

P

Papert, S., 24, 26
Paris, S., 30, 46
Patterson, C. J., 2, 29-46, 47n

Paul, B., 2, 61-79
Pea, R. D., 1-2, 5-27, 30, 41, 62
Perspective taking, in communication, 32, 34-35
Peters, R. S., 64, 78
Peterson, C. L., 36, 42, 45
Piaget, J., 1, 4, 58, 59, 60, 78
Pine, F., 48, 60
Plan construction: concept of, 6, 10-13, 20-21; cycles in, 11-12; and decision making, 12
Plan execution, concept of, 6, 13
Plan simulation, role of, 10-11
Planners, prototypic, 17-18
Planning: and attachment, mother-child, 47-60; cases of, 15-17; characteristics of, 30-31; children's perspectives on, 14-23; and communication skills, 29-46; concept of, 6-14; consequences of not, 19; constraints on, 9-10, 16-17; defined, 1, 6, 7, 31, 83; development of, 5-27; difficulty of, 21-22; flexibility in, 12-13; goal selection related to, 15-16, 41; help with, 22-23; issues in, 3; for joining play, 61-79; and multiple goals, 43-44; periods for, in communication, 43; process of, remembering, 13-14; research directions for, 23-25; ritual and creative, 18-19; and separation behavior, 47-60; social, 61-79; and social role play, 81-101; steps in, 6-7; transfer of, 24
Planning problem, representing, 6, 7-10
Plans, better and worse, distinguished, 19-20
Polson, P. G., 25
Polya, G., 10, 26
Pratt, M. W., 35, 38, 39, 42, 45
Pribram, K. H., 1, 4, 7, 26, 30, 45, 59, 60, 78
Problem state, defining, 9
Putallaz, M., 63, 65, 66, 68, 78

R

Rasmussen, B., 30, 45
Reif, F., 24, 26
Roberts, R. J., Jr., 2, 29-46
Robinson, E. J., 37, 38, 45-46
Robinson, M., 23, 25, 62, 78
Robinson, W. P., 37, 38, 46
Rogers, A., 78
Role play. *See* Social role play

S

Sacerdoti, E. D., 10, 26
Sachs, J., 84, 88, 101
Scaffolds: in communication, 42, 43; in planning, 23
Schank, R. C., 10, 26
Schmidt, C., 30, 46
Schutz, A., 7, 26
Schwartz, J. C., 47, 60
Schwartzman, H., 90, 101
Scribner, S., 35, 45
Self-other relations, in social role play, 83
Sequential combination, in social role play, 82-83
Shantz, C. U., 34, 46, 49, 60
Shatz, M., 40, 42, 46
Sheingold, K., 5n, 15, 20, 26
Shotter, J., 64, 78
Siegler, R. S., 9, 26, 62, 78
Simon, H., 7, 9, 14, 20, 25, 26
Singer, J. B., 38, 46
Smith, P., 78
Social planning: analysis of, 61-79; background on, 61-64; discussion of, 74-77; and entry episodes, 64-66; functional aspects of, 72, 75-76; methods of research on, 66-71; midgame moves in, 70-71, 74; morphological coding of, 67-69; and motivation, 73, 74-75; opening moves in, 69-70, 73-74, 76; results of study on, 71-74; and risk, 65-66, 72, 75; sequential coding of, 69-71; sex differences in, 66, 72, 73, 74, 76; structural aspects of, 72-73, 75
Social role play: analysis of, 81-101; background of, 81-84; conclusions on, 98-100; content categories in, 84-87; conventions of, 89, 90, 97; development of, 90-98; enactment techniques in, 87-88; fantasy roles in, 85, 86; frame breaks in 89-90; functional roles in, 84-85, 91-92, 93, 96-97, 99; and in-role speech, 87-88, 90, 94, 98, 99; occupational roles in, 84-85; production and regulation techniques in, 88-90; relational roles in, 84, 85, 91-92, 93-94, 95-96, 99-100; transformation in, 88-89, 97-98
Sonnenschein, S., 33, 34, 46
Speakers: and communication breakdowns, 35-36; components of skills of, 32-36; elements of message ordered by, 35; and message contents, 33-35; role knowledge by, 32; and stimulus attributes, 32-33
Speer, J. R., 44
Spencer Foundation, 5n, 47n, 81n
Stefik, M., 7, 11, 12, 26
Sullivan, H. S., 66, 76, 78

T

Thompson, G. L., 9, 26
Thorndyke, P. W., 13, 26
Travis, P. E., 44
Tuma, D. T., 24, 26
Turner, A. A., 25

U

Ungerer, J., 93, 101
Urbain, E. S., 24, 26, 42, 43, 46
Urberg, K. A., 57, 60

V

VanDevender, T. L., 50, 60
Vurpillot, E., 33, 46
Vygotsky, L. S., 11, 23, 24, 26

W

Wall, B., 78
Wall, S., 59
Wapner, S., 5n, 6, 26
Waters, E., 59
Weinraub, M., 48, 60
Weisberg, R., 31, 33, 45
Wellman, H. M., 30, 45
Werner, H., 12, 26
Wertsch, J., 23, 26
White, S., 5n
Whitehurst, G. J., 33, 34, 36, 45, 46
Whiting, B., 68, 76, 78
Whittington, S., 84, 100
Wiest, J., D., 9, 26
Wilensky, R., 7, 12, 26
Winner, E., 83, 101
Wittig, B. A., 51, 59
Wright, J. C., 44

Z

Zelazo, P., 101

Statement of Ownership, Management, and Circulation
(Required by 39 U.S.C. 3685)

1. Title of Publication: New Directions for Child Development. A. Publication number: 494-090. 2. Date of filing: 9/30/81. 3. Frequency of issue: quarterly. A. Number of issues published annually: four. B. Annual subscription price: $35 institutions; $21 individuals. 4. Location of known office of publication: 433 California Street, San Francisco (San Francisco County), California 94104. 5. Location of the headquarters or general business offices of the publishers: 433 California Street, San Francisco (San Francisco County), California 94104. 6. Names and addresses of publisher, editor, and managing editor: publisher—Jossey-Bass Inc., Publishers, 433 California Street, San Francisco, California 94104; editor—William Damon, Department of Psychology, Clark University, Worcester, Mass. 01610; managing editor—William E. Henry, 433 California Street, San Francisco, California 94104. 7. Owner: Jossey-Bass Inc., Publishers, 433 California Street, San Francisco, California 94104. 8. Known bondholders, mortgages, and other security holders owning or holding 1 percent or more of total amount of bonds, mortgages, or other securities: same as No. 7. 10. Extent and nature of circulation: (Note: first number indicates average number of copies of each issue during the preceding 12 months; the second number indicates the actual number of copies published nearest to filing date.) A. Total number of copies printed (net press run): 1638, 1604. B. Paid circulation, 1) Sales through dealers and carriers, street vendors, and counter sales: 85, 40. 2) Mail subscriptions: 535, 516. C. Total paid circulation: 620, 556. D. Free distribution by mail, carrier, or other means (samples, complimentary, and other free copies): 125, 125. E. Total distribution (sum of C and D): 745, 681. F. Copies not distributed, 1) Office use, left over, unaccounted, spoiled after printing: 893, 923. 2) Returns from news agents: 0, 0. G. Total (sum of E, F1, and 2—should equal net press run shown in A): 1638, 1604. I certify that the statements made by me above are correct and complete.

JOHN R. WARD
Vice-President

Ministry of Education, Ontario
Information Centre, 13th Floor,
Mowat Block, Queen's Park,
Toronto, Ont.   M7A 1L2